...Finding "Peace" For Your Journey

...Finding...

"Peace"

For Your Journey

In The ..."Word"... of God

In Spite of "Bitterness & Anger"

By **Melody Favor**

A Gift of "Healing" From God

Author of Little ..."Imperfect"... Inspirational

"Spiritual" Workbooks

Designed To ..."Win Souls"... To Jesus Christ
...Our "Perfect" Savior...

...Finding "Peace" For Your Journey

Who... Gets The Glory?

Almighty God!

The Father...... The Son...... The Holy Spirit......

ISBN- 978 - 0615936987
Published By
Displaying God's Anointing

Melody Favor Ministries
P.O. Box 54173
Atlanta GA, 30308
www.melodyfavor.org
email-power2press@yahoo.com

Copyright 8-2010 by Melody Favor
All Rights Reserved Unless designed otherwise,
scripture quotations are from the King James
Version of the Bible and the Amplified Version.

Printed In The United States of America
Contents and or cover may not be reproduced
in whole or in part in any form without the express
written consent of the Publisher.

In "Him" We Have **"PEACE"**

...Finding "Peace" For Your Journey

This Powerful Book Belongs To

Name _____

Presented On This Very Special Day

Date _____

Presented By This Very Special Person

_____

"Pray" ...To The FATHER ... Always For
The "Author" of This Powerful Book, Who Is
"Encouraging" You To "Invite"...Jesus Christ...Into Your Life
At Anytime While "Reading" It

...I'm Looking Forward To "Signing" Your Book...

...When We Meet ...

...On Your "Faith" Journey...

...Finding "Peace" For Your Journey

...This **"Powerful"** Little Book...
Is Just One of The ..."5"... Gifts of Favor
Books

God Has Given Me As A "Kingdom Assignment"
To "Write" To His People

...Look What's Coming Next...

"Peace"
- ➢ Strength ...For Your Journey
- ➢ Hope ...For Your Journey
- ➢ Courage ...For Your Journey
- ➢ Joy ...For Your Journey

Do You Know Someone ..."Incarcerated"...
Trying To ..."Read & Understand"...
The ..."Entire Bible"... All Alone
In Search For A ..."Little More Peace"....
Until God ..."Opens"...
The Doors And Let Them Go HOME?

They ..."left home"... one day and never got a chance to "return or pack" for their journey. Didn't kiss their love ones good-bye or take anything "extra" not even a "bible" with them for "peace" ...of mind...

...Finding "Peace" For Your Journey

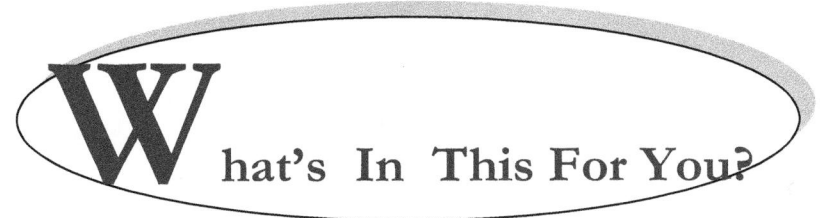

What's In This For You?

...Contents...

Let's Get Started **"Finding** Peace"....................................pg. 6

Who's "Praying" For You?..pg. 18

Who's "Peace" Do You Need?...pg. 23
Who Are You "Blaming" For Your "Bitterness & Anger?".....pg. 28

...Something You Should Know...About... ....pg. 37

The Author...	* Melody Favor....................pg. 38
The Anointed One...	* Jesus Christ ....pg. 47
The Assurance of Your	* Prayers..............................pg. 50
The Acceptance of Your	* "Faith" Journey....................pg. 55

For The Next ...32 Days... Try "Meditating On"
These Powerful Scriptures of "Peace"........................pg. 62

Peace For ....Days 1-10...pg. 76
Peace For ....Days 11-20...pg. 19
Peace For ....Days 21-32..pg. 152

Is This The End or The Beginning?..................................pg. 209

Only "Believe"...God...Will Help You "Press On" In Spite of Any
..."Bitterness or Anger"...

...To Find "Peace" For Your Journey ...In His "Word" ....

...Finding "Peace" For Your Journey

*

And the **"Peace"** of God, which passeth all **understanding** shall keep your hearts and minds through **Christ Jesus**

(Philippians 4:7)

...Finding "Peace" For Your Journey

> In The Beginning Was The ..."Word"...
> And The ... **"Word"** ... Was With God
> Always On His ..."Faith"...Journey

✱

"Meditating On"... God's Word

Will Do Many ..."Great Things"... For You Daily!

- ❖ Quiet Your Spirit...
- ❖ Purify Your Heart...
- ❖ Increase You Faith...
- ❖ Clarify Your Direction...
- ❖ Sharpen Your Perception...
- ❖ Enlarge Your View of God...
- ❖ Confirm Your Cautions of Counsel...

Guide You To Success ... On Your **"Faith"** Journey

✱

Finally, brethren, farwell.
Be perfect, be of good comfort, be of one mind, live in
"Peace" and the God of love and **"Peace"**
shall be with you.
Greet one another in **"Faith"** on your journey
with an holy kiss.
(2 Corinthians 13: 11-12)

...Finding "Peace" For Your Journey

Adding **"Peace"** To Your Journey

A Few "Good' Reasons To "Press On" To Walk In The "Peace" of God For Life

➢ **God Loves You...**
For God so loved the world, that he gave his only begotten Son, that whosoever believed in him should not perish, but have everlasting life
...**John 3:16**

But God commendeth his love toward us, in that while we were yet sinners, Christ died for us. ...**Romans 5:8**

➢ **All Are Sinners...**
For all have sinned, and come short of the glory of God.
...**Romans 3:23**

As it is written, There is none righteous, no, not one.
...**Romans 3:10**

➢ **God's Remedy for Sin...**
For the wages of sin is death: but the gift of God is eternal life through Jesus Christ our Lord. ...**Romans 6:23**

But as many as received him, to them gave he power to become the sons of God, even to them that believe on his name. ...**John 1:12**

➢ **All May Be Saved...**
Behold, I stand at the door, and knock: if any man hear my voice, and open the door, I will come in to him. ...**Revelation 3:20**

➢ **Assurance As A Believer**
But, these are written, that ye might believe that Jesus is the Christ, the Son of God: and that believing ye might have life through his name.
...**John 20:31**

...Finding "Peace" For Your Journey

More "Peace" For Your Journey

...In The ..."Midst"... of Any Storm ... "Meditate On"...

When you are sad,………………………………………………………. John 14

When you have sinned,………………………………………………Psalms 51

When you are facing danger,………………………………………Psalms 91

When people have failed you,……………………………………Psalms 27

When feeling God is far from you,……………………………. Psalms 139

When your faith needs stirring up,……………………………Hebrews 11

When you are alone and scared,………………………………Psalms 23

When you are worried,……………………………………………Matt. 8:19-34

When feeling hurt by man's love,………………………………1 Cor. 13

When you wonder about Christianity,………………….…2 Cor. 5:15-18

When you feel like an outcast,……………………………….Romans 8:1-39

When you are leaving home for a trip,………………….…..Psalm s 121

When your bank account is empty,………………………….Psalms 37

When you want to carry fruit, ……………………………………John 15

When you need a healing for your soul,…………………Psalms 103

...Finding "Peace" For Your Journey

God's "Purpose"
...For This Little Imperfect Book...

...Written April – July 2010...

➢ <u>To Help **"Win Souls"**</u>

To The ...Kingdom of God...

By Offering Our ..."Lord & Savior"...
"Jesus Christ"
To You By Sharing ..."His Word"...

And I, if I be "lifted up" from the earth,
Will ..."draw all"... men unto me.
(John 12:32)

➢ <u>To Help **"Inspire"** Others</u>

... "Motivate & Encourage" ...

You To Write Your "Own" Little "Imperfect" Book

...Trusting In The LORD... with all thine heart; and lean not unto thine own understanding. In all thy ways "acknowledge him" and he shall direct thy path.
(Proverbs 3:5-6)

God's "Purpose"
...For The Author...

You Will Not "Believe" What Great

"Peace" & Healing

I "Find" being in the "Presence" of the LORD each day. In His "WORD" all day!

When He's speaking to me about what to "write" unto His People, for Him, I get excited, get still and I have to listen carefully to make sure it's all about Him, and His Glory. Remember, the word says Jesus, learned obedience through the things he suffered.

...So Am I... (Hebrews 5:8) So Can You!

Some days it's very painful, because of the Lupus. My hands hurt and swell, but I keep on "pressing on" to pray, study, worship, type, fast to "obey" what my Father has instructed me to do for Him, in spite of my P.A.I.N. and mental illness. I LOVE Him!

...Read (Jer. 30:2-3) & (Isaiah 55:7-12)...

...Finding "Peace" For Your Journey

God's "Purpose"...For You...

*

Thou will keep him in perfect "peace" whose mind is strayed on thee: because he trusteth in thee.

Trust ye in the LORD for ever: for in the LORD JEHOVAH us everlasting: strength

(Isaiah 26:3-4)

...Finding "Peace" For Your Journey

God's "Purpose"...For Us....

Depart from **evil,** and do good: **seek** **"peace"** and pursue it. The **eyes** of the LORD are upon the **righteous** and his **ears** are unto their **cry.**

(Psalms 34:14-15)

...Finding "Peace" For Your Journey

...Now I ..."Speak"

"Peace" To Your Painful Storms!

In The ...Mighty... Name of

"Jesus"

I ..."Decree & Declare"... You Too Shall "Live" And "Not Die" In The ..."Midst"... of Your Storms.

So Shall You "Speak" of His **"Perfect"**

P...Power he gave you to "defeat" all of your enemies

E...Everlasting "covenants" and promises to endure

A...Acceptance into His "Kingdom" through His Son

C...Comfort of His "Holy Spirit" leading you day & night

E...Erased all of your "sins" by the shedding of his blood

Have Peace On Your "Faith" Journey ... Knowing He Will ... "Carry You" Through It All ... All The Way Home

...To Be With The Father...

...Finding "Peace" For Your Journey

...Now I ..."Pray"

by the "awesome" power of the "Most High God" something you will "read" in this "powerful" little book will help the Lord "draw you closer" to him for

...His Purpose and His Plan...

If only... He can seize just a moment of your time to

..."reveal" himself to you...

like He did for me when I was 28 years.

I'm praying you will let him ..."add"... a little

"Peace" to your "Faith" journey ... in the midst of your storm like he's "adding" to mines right now,
...Tuesday May 4th, 2010...

...without it... you will not be able to...

"Recognize" "Relate" "Realize" "Receive"

His Great ..."Love"... for you on your soon to be

..."Faith" Journey...

as he personally escorts you to the "Cross" like He did His Son Jesus Christ ...The Anointed One...

when he was here on earth on ...His "Faith" Journey...

...Finding "Peace" For Your Journey

Many may be in the midst of a "Painful-Storm" a new
"Change" about to "come over" them!

They now find themselves **"locked-up"** in
a "jail cell" with many strangers, angry, frustrated,
afraid and feeling, all alone inside.
They immediately start asking the question

*

How Did I Let ..."**Myself**"...
Get In This ..."**Mess?**"...

*

How Am I Going To Get **"Myself"** Out Of
This ..."**Bad**"... Situation?

Soon **blaming** or questioning God.

Asking why, did He **"let this"** happen to them?
Now needing and "praying" that
"someone" anyone, would quickly
..."help them" ... "deal" with their new P.A.I.N.
...Pressures...Addictions...Insecurities...Needs...

...Finding "Peace" For Your Journey

That's Where

...Melody Favor Ministries...
Comes In
We Are Here To Share The "Word" of God
To "HelpU" Find "Strength" For Your Journey

*

"Power2Press" On Through Your P.A.I.N.
..."To Live Life On Purpose"...
No Matter ..."Where You Are"... Right Now!

We Will "HelpU" Find The
Strength...Peace...Hope...Courage...Joy

You Will "Need" On Your "FAITH" Journey
In The ..."WORD"... of God
To Help You ..."Reach"... Your Divine Destination
As You ..."Meditate On"...
...God's Word...
And
"Press On"... To Do His Will

Who's ... Praying For You...

Greetings ... my dear sister or brother in Christ, by the "Grace of God"...you are about to be empowered by **"The Truth"** It Teaches... Restores... Unites... Transforms... Heals... all things with... **"The Word of God"** ... by Faith. Thank you for your love and support each time you purchase any of our **Christian Books** and **CD's** or have the opportunity to attend our powerful conferences, weekly and monthly gatherings in the future.

We Are "Praying"...that after you've enjoyed them and hopefully been blessed and strengthened by them we are "praying" that you'll be led to "share" our products to love ones, friends and even your enemies. By doing this you are helping us to keep our **"True Commitment"** to God and the **"True Vision"** of this powerful "Healing Ministry" to sharing the Gospel of Jesus Christ worldwide to help "Win Souls" to Christ and to further advance, The Kingdom of God.

We Are "Praying"...for you as you seek to find "Peace" for your journey, to reach your divine destination or to fulfill your divine "Purpose In Life." **God's "Perfect Will"** for you will never led you where God's Grace can not keep you in Perfect Peace.

We Are "Praying" ...that you will **"Receive"** by the ..."**Grace of God"**... everything your **"Heavenly Father"** has predestined for you to have on this earth, before you were even born, while you were still forming in your mother's womb.

We Are "Praying" ...that your **"True Healing"** begin time you choose to **"Believe"** that your **Heavenly Father** had you in mind when He encouraged me to write this powerful little book. He knew some way... somehow... He would "use" someone special, traveling on your path to put it in your **"Praying Hands"** just when you would **"need it"** the most. You are blessed to be alive and see the **"Peace of God"** be added to your **"Faith Journey."**

We Are "Praying" ...that your **"Faith In God"** will be increased even the more as you **"Meditate On"** on God's Word and choose to ..."**Believe"**... in God The Father...The Son... and The Holy Spirit... with your whole heart while traveling on your **"Faith Journey"** with them all. They will never fail you.

We Are "Praying" ...that you will be **"Inspired"** to search for the ..."**True Meaning"**... of each powerful word of scripture written in this book. This deeper level of studying the scriptures for yourself will empower you with the **"Revelation"** you need in order to help you ..."**apply" God's Word**... of Peace, Strength, Guidance and Healing to the current issues you're facing.

✱

We Are "Praying"...this book ...**Finding "Peace" For Your Journey**... and the other **"Journey Books"** to come, will motivate and encourage you to seek for more **of God's "wisdom and guidance"** by making time to read your **"Holy Bible."** By doing this **"Daily"** it will help you become a more **"Spiritually ...Minded...Mature...Christian."** One who learns how to call on the one who's able to **keep you from falling and quitting** when the **"Storms of Life"... starts "Raging"** and it seems to be "No Way Out". **You will learn the..."power of choosing"...to "Walk By Faith"** and not by sight, trusting totally in The Only Wise God.

We Are "Praying"...that your **"Fear"** of failing **God,** others and even yourselves due to the painful issues that are **"oppressing and depressing"** you daily will eventually "cause you" even the more to ...call on... The **"Only Wise God"** daily as you travel on your "Faith" journey. His name is **Jehovah Jireh the "Lord God My Provider."** His Son's name is Jesus. They are both **"able and ready"** to "help you" reach your destination on time and safe in their arms, by the power of the **"Holy Spirit."**

We Are "Praying"...that you be **"Encouraged"** by my **"Painful-Powerful"** testimony and that it becomes the **"Proof"** you need to prove there are many "Treasures" in your trials too. **My Heart's Desire is to "Speak"** a few words of **"Healing"** into your heart to give you the **"Strength"** you need to **"Keep Pressing On"** to do ...God's Will... in spite of your **"P.A.I.N."** Believe me, they tried to "stop me" too. But, The Love of God ...The Will of God...The Purpose of God...The Word of God... The Peace of God wouldn't let the enemy "Defeat" or stop me!

...Finding "Peace" For Your Journey

We Are "Praying"

...For You...

that by the **"Grace"** of the living God...
if after reading this powerful **"little book"** if the only powerful "scripture" you'll able to **"remember"** and

"Meditate On" ...is this one...

(Isaiah 26:3-4)

Thou will keep thee in **"Perfect Peace"**

whose **mind**...is stayed on thee...

because **he** trusteth in thee;

Trust ye...in the **Lord for ever**...

for in the Lord JEHOVAH is

everlasting strength.

Our ..."Prayers"... Would Be Answered.

We Are "Praying"

...For The...

"Peace" of God

to be with you once you ..."find It"...until the end of ...Your "Faith" Journey...

*

...It's Your Choice To **"SEEK"** ...

...The **"Peace of God"**... Daily By Choosing To

..."Search"... "Expect"... "Embrace"... "Keep"...

Building Your "Faith" ... In The Word of God...

... If You Confess & Think "PAIN" Daily ...

You Will Have More "P.A.I.N." Than More "PEACE"

Learn To ..."**Meditate On**"...

God's Word ... Daily On ...Your "Faith" Journey

...Finding "Peace" For Your Journey

*

...Who's... "Peace" Do You Need?

*

...Peace I leave with you...

"My Peace"

I give unto you... not as the world giveth,

give I unto you...

Let not your **heart be troubled** neither let it be **afraid.**
(John 14:27) KJ

..."Peace"...

When I think of how many times on my journey, I've allowed others to steal my "Peace" and my "Joy." It really was causing me to have a lot of so "Bitterness & Anger" in my heart towards myself and others, even people that I knew I loved and they loved me.

However by the grace of God I soon discovered by spending more time in "His Word" they didn't steal anything but time. That's right time. No! They didn't steal anything from me ... I gave my "Peace" to them.

The time it took for me to stand there and realize I was wrong to even worry about things I have no control over or things I could have handle differently was a waste of my time. I needed to learn how to take it to the Lord in prayer, let it go and keep moving in spite of my issues that were trying to make me quit on God or slow me down with feelings of defeat.

...Finding "Peace" For Your Journey

I Should Have "Trusted"
And ..."Meditated On"...
The ..."Word"... of God

(1 Peter 5: 7)

Casting all "my cares" upon him; for

he careth for me.

*

This Is How "Easy" It Will Be To Enjoy Reading

...This Little Book...

...It's Not Deep... It's Simply "Filled With" The Word of God

To Help You Find

A Word of "PEACE" Quickly When You Need It. The Most.

To Help You "Keep Moving" On Your "Faith" Journey Daily.

And To Be Able To Share "His Peace" As You Travel

The Highways And The By Ways

*

Without Developing A "Solid" Relationship
With "Jesus Christ"

There Can Be No Real

"Peace"

For Any of Us!

...Finding "Peace" For Your Journey

And
The "Peace" of God

which passeth all understanding, shall keep your hearts and minds through Christ Jesus.

(Philippians 4:7)

Finally, brethren, whatsoever things are true, whatsoever things are honest, whatsoever things are just, whatsoever things are pure, whatsoever things are lovely, whatsoever things are of good report; if there be any virtue, and if there be any praise, think on these things.

Those things, which ye have both learned, and received, and heard, and seen in me, do: and the

God of ... "Peace" ... shall be with you.

(Philippians 4:8-9)

...Finding "Peace" For Your Journey

All God's ..."Peace"...

(shall be yours, that tranquil state of a soul assured of its salvation through Christ, and so fearing nothing from God and being content with its earthly lot of whatever sort that is, that peace) which transcends all understanding shall garrison and mount guard over your hearts and minds in

Christ Jesus.

(Philippians 4:7) KJ, amp.

For unto us a child is born, unto us a son is given: and the government shall be upon his shoulder: and his name shall be called Wonderful, Counselor, The mighty God, The everlasting Father,

The Prince of "Peace"

(Isaiah 9:6)

Always.... as long as you choose to "Serve HIM"

while you're traveling on

Your "Faith" Journey

Without "Faith" In God It's Hard To Experience "True Peace"

Who Are You "Blaming" For Your "Bitterness & Anger" On Your ..."Faith" Journey?...

"Apostle Paul" had many people on his "Faith Journey" that he could have ...blamed... daily for any "Bitterness and Anger" he may have felt when he was chosen and commissioned by God against his own will seems like way back on

the road of Damascus.

But, He didn't, not once. However, he went on to become known as one of the most "powerful witnesses" to the Gospel of Jesus Christ, even though he never walked with our Lord in the nature he encouraged others to

..."Fight The Good Fight of Faith"...

as he did until his death.

(2 Corinthians 10:2-4) amplified

I entreat you when I do come (to you) that I may not be driven to such) boldness as I intend to show toward those few who suspect us 0f acting according to the flesh (on the low level of worldly motives and as if invested with only human powers). For though we walk (live) in the flesh, we are not carrying on our warfare according to the flesh and using mere human weapons.

For the weapons of our warfare are not physical (weapons of flesh and blood), but they are mighty before God for the overthrow and destruction of strongholds.

Casting down imaginations, and every high thing that exalted itself against the knowledge of God, and bring into captivity every thought to the obedience of Christ:... (v5 KJ)

Read his powerful story ... found in the book of

...Acts 9th chapter...

Let's See How "We" Can

..."Overcome"...

"Bitterness & Anger"

By "Meditating On" The "Word" of God

- ❖ Our battle against impure thoughts is far more than some mental or physical struggle. It is spiritual warfare.

"For our struggle is not against flesh and blood, but against the rulers, against the authorities, against powers of this dark world and against the spiritual forces of evil in the heavenly realms." (Eph. 6:12)

- ❖ God knows that our natural inclinations easily betray us. They betray us to the delusive results that anger can produce in others in exchange for our destruction. God does not want us just to conquer anger; He wants us to use the pressure of the battle as "daily motivation" to transform our mind to "His way of thinking." This will be by the Holy Spirit if we give Him His weapon.

- ❖ take the sword of the Spirit, which is the "word of God."

  (Ephesians 6:17)

- ❖ It is not only important to resist temptation, but it is equally important to prepare ourselves between temptations.

- ❖ Here is a list of key Scriptures which must be in the "mind" of one who intends to conquer "Bitterness & Anger."

A fool's vexation is known at once, but a prudent man conceals dishonor.

(Proverbs 12:16)

A quick-tempered man acts foolishly, and a man of evil devices is hated.

(Proverbs 14:17)

He who is slow to anger has great understanding, but he who is quick-tempered exalts folly.

(Proverbs 14:29)

A gently answer turns away wrath, but a harsh word stirs up anger. (Proverbs 15:1)

A hot-tempered man stirs up strife, but the slow to anger pacifies contention. (Proverbs 15:18)

Let all "bitterness" and wrath and anger and clamor and slander be put away from you, along with all malice, And be kind to one another, tender-hearted, forgiving each other, just as God in Christ also has forgiven you. (Ephesians 4:22-26)

Now the deeds of the flesh are evident, which are: immorality, impurity, sensuality, idolatry, sorcery, enmities, strife, jealousy, outbursts of anger, disputes, dissensions, factions, envying, drunkenness, carousing, and things like these, of which I forewarn you just as I have forewarned you that those who practice such things shall not inherit the kingdom of God. (Galatians 5:19-21)

This you know, my beloved brethren, but let everyone be quick to hear, slow to speak and slow to anger; for the anger of man does not achieve the righteousness of God. (James 1:19-20)

Confess your sins one to another, and pray one for another, that you may be healed. The effectual, fervent prayer of a righteous man availeth much. (James 5:16)

Do not associate with a man given to anger; or go with a hot-tempered man, lest you learn his ways, and find a snare for yourself. (Proverbs 22:24-25)

❖ A sincere Christian...cannot enjoy anger unless he temporarily blots out of his consciousness the presence of God. If we knew that God was evaluating every one of our actions, we would quickly reject those which are wrong. This is precisely what the fear of the Lord is, the moment by moment awareness that God is watching and weighing every one of our words, thoughts, actions and attitudes.

God Knows All About Our "Bitterness & Anger"
...His "Word" Is Our Only Cure!...

Next Time You Feel **"Bitterness & Anger"**

...Coming Your Way.. Remember...

Thou God sees me. (Genesis 16:13)

The eyes of the Lord are in every place, beholding the evil and the good. (Proverbs 15:3)

That everyone may receive the things done in his body, according to that he hath done, whether it be good or bad. (2 Corinthians 5:10)

... Now Let's "Keep Moving" ... By FAITH...

...**"Meditating On"**... God's Word ...

And See Where "The End" Leads Us Together!

Do Not ..."Blame"... Others For Your "Bitterness & Anger"

For The ..."Word" of God... Says;

But "prove yourselves" doers of the word, and not merely "hearers" who delude themselves. For if anyone is a hearer of the word and not a doer, he is like a man who looked at himself and gone away, he has immediately forgotten what kind of person he was, but one who looks intently at the perfect law, the law of liberty, and abides by it, not having become a forgetful hearer but an effectual doer, this man shall be blessed in what he does.
(James 1:22-25)

To sum up, let all be harmonious, sympathetic, brotherly, kindhearted, and humble in spirit; not returning evil for evil, or insult for insult, but giving a blessing instead; for you were called for the very purpose that you might inherit a blessing.
(1 Peter 3:8-9)

Above all, keep fervent in your love for one another, because love covers a multitude of sins.
(1Peter 4:8)

Now Take A Moment To **"Meditate On"**

And …"Write"… Down

Some of The Things That Has Caused You

…"Bitterness & Anger"…

…On Your "Faith" Journey…

_____
_____
_____
_____
_____
_____
_____
_____
_____
_____
_____
_____
_____
_____
_____
_____
_____
_____

What Are You Going To Do "Differently" Next Time "Bitterness & Anger" Shows Up Now That God Has Giving You …His Word… To Help You Have "Peace" On Your Journey?

_____
_____
_____
_____
_____
_____
_____
_____
_____
_____
_____
_____
_____
_____
_____
_____
_____

...Finding "Peace" For Your Journey

Something... **Y**ou... **S**hould... **K**now...**A**bout...

The Author...	*	**Melody Favor**
The Anointed One...	*	**Jesus Christ**
The Assurance of Your	*	**Prayers**
The Acceptance of Your	*	**"Faith" Journey**

*

"We pray" ...knowing more about... **"us"**
will **"Strengthen & Encourage"**
you to keep praying to ...**God**... asking him to
"add" the **"Peace"** you'll need daily

*

to keep you ..."moving"... in the "direction"
you ...**"believe he's leading"**... you to
in spite of any
...**"Bitterness & Anger"**...
...you may encounter...

*

...**On Your "Faith" Journey**...

37

...Finding "Peace" For Your Journey

...The Author...
Melody Favor

I'm not a ..."Famous Author"... (yet) or a "Professional Doctor" qualified to tell you ...what's really causing you...

"Bitterness & Anger"

I'm someone who's blessed to "share" with you how the power of "God's Word"..."Heals My P.A.I.N."

Pressures... Addictions...Insecurities...Needs...

Just sharing the "Word of God" to others often "adds" so much "PEACE" to my "Faith" journey when I'm faced with "Bitterness & Anger" of my own.

Throughout this book I share a little of my testimony in hopes to strengthen and encourage you to put your "Trust In God" and in ..."His Word" ...to help you

"Keep Moving ... Walking In Faith."

...Finding "Peace" For Your Journey

God simply placed a "burning"

"Desire In My Heart"

to share ... **"His Word"** ...

to the ...world... in hopes to "Win Souls" to Christ and to "Strengthen" others back in 2002 when I wrote my "first book."

Especially to those who are **"LOCKED UP"**
...for real...

"Feeling" ...Hopeless...Afraid...Stuck...Unworthy...

of God's "Grace & Mercy" his "Love & Help."

Feeling all alone. Afraid that no one really

cares or even "understands"

how their "life" has taking a sudden "wrong" turn into

A "Bitter & Angry"

...Dark & Weary Place...

*

Grandma and all church going "old folks"
over the years of my life has taught me to say
I'm A "Sinner" ...Saved... By Grace!

And that I should **"Love"** the **"Lord"** her God...their God with my whole **"Heart."**

Well I fail short? I didn't stay "saved" ...all my life...

I ..."fail down"... many times and had to find

"My God!... My Way!...For Myself!"

I started remembering how "good" he had been to me and my "dysfunctional family." Praying he was still be as good to me today as he had in the past.

<u>He Is Still Our ..."Faithful" God... Today!</u>

He's "Never" Forsaken My Kids "Larry & Danielle."

He Still "Whispers" To Me Daily

..."Daughter Only Believe"...

The "Best" Is Yet To Come!

For You & Your "Whole Family"

Just Keep The "Faith" ...Lose The Fear...

On Your Journey ... And I'll "Walk With You All"

And Help Each of You ..."Fight"...

The ..."Good Fight of Faith"... Until The End!

..."Better Days ... Did Come"...

For Us... "Several Times"...

Many times we had to humble ourselves and

"turn away" from sin and back to ...Christ" for real...

Ask Him once again to "forgive us of all my sins"

with a real sense of "understanding" that He will.

Knowing He's the "only one" who can help us
face our "Bitterness & Anger" through prayer, and

...Finding "Peace" In His Word...

...On My Journey...

I had so much **"Bitterness & Anger"** in my heart after the death of my only brother Danny, who passed away March 3rd, 1989 with aids. I got high for seven months straight. Finally by September 1989 I was so tired of getting high and playing church, I wanted out of that foolish game, that "death" even became an "option." I remember reading somewhere in the bible about "Walking In The Fullness of Christ"

and that's what I wanted all along, but didn't know how to "pursue it" or to stop doing wrong long enough to find it. But The Lord had others placed in my life that kept "preaching" the gospel to me, until I finally got it! Amen!!! Today Friday July 30, 2010, at 11:33am, the Lord is leading me to come back and "add" this extra little testimony to give you "Peace"

...Finding "Peace" For Your Journey

...about me...

"Melody Favor"

I'm indeed a sinner "saved by grace."

Now at age fifty one I can say what "Apostle Paul"

said and mean it too!

(Romans 1:16-17)

For I am not ashamed of the gospel of Christ:

for it is the power of God unto salvation to everyone that believeth; to the Jews first, and also to the Greek.

For therein is the righteousness of God revealed from Faith to faith: as it is written,

The just shall live by faith...

...My "Faith" Journey...

Has lasted thus far ..."51"... long years
by the "Grace" of God.
There are so many things that I could share about
"my life" that would make you say... Oh My God,
he allowed you to go through all of that just so you

would be "anointed" to write these "little" imperfect books. Usually, when a person begins to speak of themselves they seem to want the hearer or the reader to know all the "Great Things" about their wonderful life. You know, the ones that makes others often time "wish" it was their life story of

"Great Successes."

Like the love able family members, many masters, bachelors, doctorial degree they have, and all the different boards and committee they are on and numerous awards and outstanding accomplishments they've been recognized for over their life time.

Well I'm not saying any of that is wrong. I'm very happy when I read the awesome "Bios" of famous people that God has often used. That's just not my story, my "experience" or my awesome "Bio."

Thanks Be To God... I'm just now realizing at age fifty one as I come back to type "this page" of the book on this beautiful Monday morning, July 6th, 2010, that many of the things I was just calling bad, ugly, shameful, unhappy discouraging, unfair on "My Faith Journey" was indeed God's "Perfect Will" for me. And It's not too late for me to tell Him "Thank You LORD".. for not forsaking me.

God has just given me a "Powerful Word" on Sunday July 4th , to let me know, that He has "personally" had His "Hand On Me" the "whole time" since He called me into ministry at my mother's funeral April 4th 1990...during the good, bad and the ugly places.

and that my **"Bitterness & Anger"**

has worked for ..."His Good"...

I have tears in my eyes right now just thinking about how **"Faithful"** ...**God has been to me** and my dysfunctional family on "our journey" even when I didn't see it as a ..."Faith" Journey... it was more like a "Missed Up" Journey ...
if you know what I mean.
But
To God Be The "Glory"
for the many "painful" things He's brought us through.

God's ..."Perfect Will"... for me has given me something that money and degrees couldn't buy me on my "Faith Journey. It has given me so many wonderful and painful **"experiences"** along the way.

I share a few of them with you through-out the book. I've been standing on this powerful scripture for over seven years or longer, when I was about to lose my home to foreclosure, cars to reposition , my mind to "bi-polar" and crack almost killed me when it exploded in my body.

As you can see I have many "degrees of issues." I've recently earned my "Doctorial" in the understanding of this "powerful word" of truth from God.

...(1 Peter 5:10)...

But the "God of all Grace"
who hath called us unto his eternal glory by

Christ Jesus,

after that ye have "suffered" a while

make you perfect, stablish, strengthen, settle you.

To Him be glory and dominion for ever and ever. Amen. I pray it will encourage you to

"Trust God" each day and to ask Him to "add" a word of **"Peace"** daily from His Word to help you Keep You "Moving"
On Your ..."Faith" Journey...
in spite of "Your Bitterness & Your Anger."

...Finding "Peace" For Your Journey

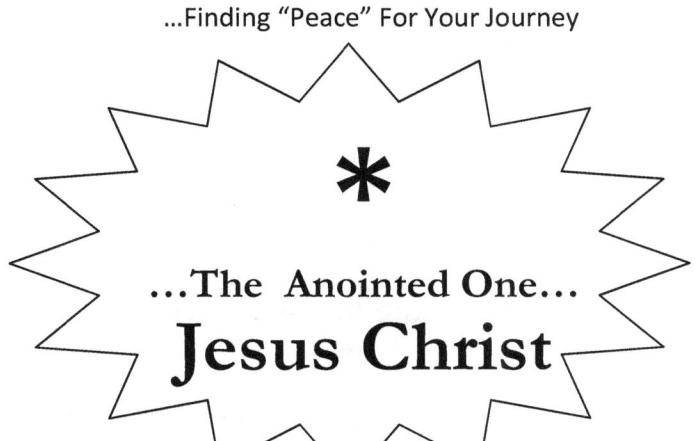

...The Anointed One...
Jesus Christ

The Way... The Truth... The Life...

His "Journey"

Led Him To The ..."Cross"... To Died For ...

...You And I...

(Matthew 12:1-23)

Now the birth of ...**Jesus Christ**...

was on this wise: When as his mother Mary was espoused to Joseph, before they came together, she was found with child of the Holy Ghost.

Then Joseph her husband,, being a just man, and not willing to make her away privily.

But while he thought on these things, behold, the angel of the Lord appeared unto him in a dream, saying, Joseph, thou son of David, fear not to take unto thee Mary thy wife: for that which is conceived in her is of the Holy Ghost.

And she shall bring forth a son, and thou shalt call his name Jesus: for he shall ... **"SAVE"** ... his people from their sins.

Now all this was done, that it might be fulfilled which was spoken of the Lord by the prophet, saying,

Behold, a virgin shall be with child, and shall bring forth a son, and the shall call his name Emmanuel, which being interpreted is, God with us.

...Finding "Peace" For Your Journey

He Came Unto Us As The "Great"

...I AM...

God	(John 17:3)
Father	(Psalms 68:5)
Master	(John 13:13)
Healer	(Isaiah 53:5)
Savior	(Isaiah 43:3)
Deliverer	(Daniel 3:17)
Redeemer	(Ephesians 1:7)
Resurrection	(John 11:25)
LORD of LORDS	(Revelation 19:16)
The "King" of Glory	(Psalms 24:8)
The "Rejected" Stone	(Psalm 118:22)
The Prince of "Peace"	(Isaiah 9:6)
The "Good" Shepherd	(John 10:11)

Check Off

...Who He Is To You...

...Finding "Peace" For Your Journey

...The Assurance of...
Your Prayers

Starts First With You Choosing To

*

"Believe"

..."Prayer"... Changes Things...

*

God **"Answers Prayers"** According To His Word!

You Must Learn To ..."**Declare & Decree**"...

His "Promises" ... Back To Him... In "Prayer"

And Pray Them In The ...Name of ..."**Jesus**"...

Learn To Pray For... The **Father's Will**

To Be Done "For You" Always According To ...His Word...

There will be times when you're walking right along and having a great day. And all of a sudden you're overwhelmed by the feelings of resentment,

"Bitterness & Anger"

You start to feel down, sad, oppressed and depress, they all seem to come alive at once out of nowhere…the grave, the dead file.

And they are placing "demands" on you and your emotions, that you are "forced" to pray but, can not seem to find the "right words" to pray to keep the

"Peace" of God… you had before they came to

"play" with your "mind" and to keep you moving forward …if only just for that day…say quit…

take a break… it's too hard!

Don't listen to them… keep "moving by faith" in the spirit of love. Hurry up and find you a bible, open it

up to the book of … **"Psalms"** …

and begin to "pray" what David …prayed…

Always ..."Meditate On"...
"God's Word"

And "Remember" How Often God Delivered

...King David... And Others Out of His

..."Many" Troubles...

I Know ...He'll Do The Same For You...

Be pleased, O Lord, to deliver me:
O Lord, make haste to help me.
(Psalms 40:13) KJ

I WAITED patiently for the Lord; and he inclined, unto me, and heard me cry. He brought me up also out of an horrible pit, out of the miry clay, and set my feet upon a rock, and established my goings.
And he hath put a new song in my mouth, ever praise unto our God many shall see it, and fear,
and shall trust in the Lord.

Blessed is that man that maketh the Lord his trust, and respecteth not the proud, nor such as turn aside to lies.
Many, O Lord my God, are thy wonderful works which thou hast done, and thy thoughts which are to us-ward: they cannot be reckoned up in order unto thee if I would declare and
speak of them,
they are more that can be numbered.
(Psalms 40:1-5) KJ

Let them be ashamed and confounded together that seek after my soul to destroy it; let them be driven backward and put to shame that wish me evil. Let them be desolate for a reward of their shame that say unto me, Aha, aha.
(Psalm 40: 14) KJ
But I am poor and needy; yet the Lord thinketh upon me: thou art my help and my deliver; make no tarrying
O my God.
(Psalms 40:17) KJ

...Finding "Peace" For Your Journey

After "Praying" Many Times
...To My Father...
He Often ...Answers Me... By Saying... Remember

"Daughter"

For I know the thoughts and plans
that I have for you,
says the Lord,
thoughts and plans for welfare and "Peace"

and not for evil, to give you hope in your final outcome.

Then you will call upon Me, and you will come and

"Pray" to Me, and I will hear and heed you.

Then you will seek Me, inquire for, and require Me

(as a vital necessity) and find Me when you search for Me with all your heart. And I will be found of you,

saith the Lord:

and I will turn away your captivity,

and I will gather you from all the nations, and from all the places whither I have driven you, saith the Lord;

and I will bring you again into the place whence I caused you to be carried away captive. (Jer. 29:1-14) j

...Finding "Peace" For Your Journey

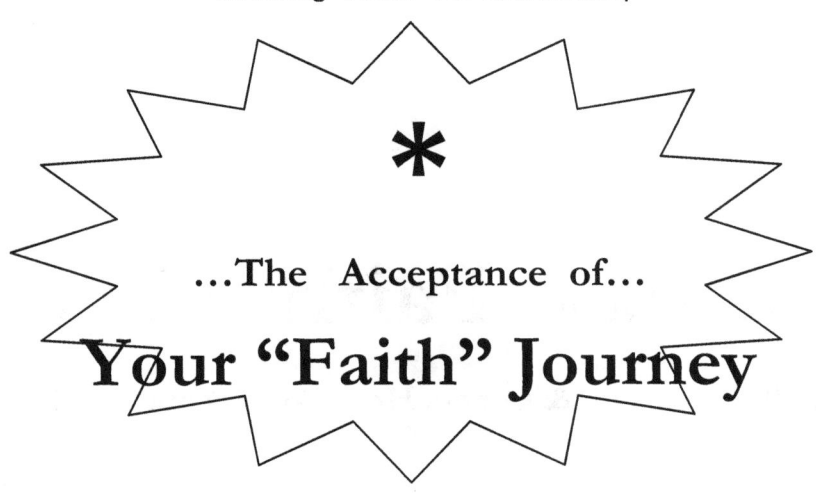

...The Acceptance of...
Your "Faith" Journey

One of The ..."Most Important"...
Things You Will Need To **"Accept"**
...On Your "Faith" Journey...

...Is "God" Wants To Have ...

"Total Control"

...Of Your "New Life"....

To Use It ... For His Purpose... And ...His Plan...
...To Bring Him "All" The Glory...
...And To Draw All Men Unto Him...

...Finding "Peace" For Your Journey

Your New "Faith" Journey

Will Teach You & Others How To "Accept" Losing

...Your Life... for Christ Sakes

Then said Jesus unto his disciples, if any man will come after me, let him deny himself, and take up his cross, and follow me. For whoever will save his life shall lose it: and whoever

...lose his life for...

my sake shall find it.

(Matthew 16:24-25)

...Finding "Peace" For Your Journey

...The Acceptance of This...
"Warning"

Will Save Your Life And The Lives Of Your "Love Ones"

...Once You "Decide" To Give...

"Your Life" To ...God...
Learn The Importance Of Being ..."Spiritually"...Sober... At All Times

...On Your "Faith" Journey...

Because the enemy...is "waiting" for you to get "drunk" and take back "control of your life" from out of the "Hands of God." Then attempt to drive yourself home while going straight to hell not heaven.

There are many "dangerous things" the enemy already has "posted up" along the roadside that you will think is leading you safely back home. However, when you run into them and they almost get you and your family

killed, you will see it was "no accident."
Their job is to stop you and catch you "sleeping"
when you should be "praying"
and paying "attention" to all the "warning signs"
saying "danger" one way street, road out up ahead,
"turn back" to the "CROSS!"
...At Least Die For "Christ Sakes"...
These traps and tricks will eventually

"ROB" you of the ..."TRUE PEACE" of God...

If you don't make time to

"Pray"...while traveling on... Your "Faith" Journey...

You must find a way to keep a "Bible" with you at
...all times...
and learn to **"Accept"** the help of the
"Holy Spirit" to guide you "safely" back home
daily through the ...**Word of God**...
Make Him Your Comforter and "Spiritual Compass."

...Finding "Peace" For Your Journey

1 **Remember** Hearing God Say To Me;
It's Time...Bring It...To Me...
...I Have Need of It...
UNTO YOU, O Lord,
do I bring my Life. O my God, I trust, lean on,
rely on, and am confident in You. Let me not be to shame or
(my hope in You) be disappointed; let not my
enemies triumph over me.
Yes, let none who trust and wait hopefully and look for You be
put to shame or be disappointed; let them be
ashamed who forsake the right or deal
treacherously without cause.
Show me Your ways, O Lord; teach me Your paths.
Guide me in Your truth and faithfulness and teach me
for You are the God of my salvation; for You (You only
and altogether) do I wait (expectantly)
all the day long.   (Psalms 25: 1-5)

(Psalms 25:7)

Remember, not the sins (the lapses and frailties) of my youth of my transgressions; according to Your mercy and steadfast love remember me, for Your goodness sake, O Lord

(Psalms 25:9-22)

He leads the humble in what is right, and the humble He teaches His way. All the paths of the Lord are mercy and steadfast love, even truth and faithfulness are they for those who keep His covenant and His testimonies.

For Your name's sake, O Lord, pardon my iniquity and my quilt, for (they are) great

(Psalms 25:12 – 22)

Who is the man who reverently fears and worships the Lord? Him shall He teach in the way that he should choose.

He himself shall dwell at ease, and his offspring shall inherit the land.

The secret (of the sweet, satisfying companionship) of
the Lord have they... on their ..."Faith" Journey...

who fear (revere and worship) Him. He will show them His
covenant and reveal to its (deep, inner) meaning

My eyes are ever toward the Lord, for He will

pluck my feet out of the net.

Lord, turn to me and be gracious to me, for I am lonely
and afflicted. The troubles of my heart are multiplied;

bring me out of my distresses. Behold my affliction and my
pain and forgive all my sins

(of thinking and doing).

Consider my enemies, for they abound; they hate me with cruel
hatred.   O keep me, Lord, and deliver me; let me not be
ashamed of disappointed, for my trust and my refuge are in
You.

Let integrity and uprightness preserve me, for

I wait for and expect You.

Redeem Israel, O God, out of all their troubles...

I Believe... Father God...By Faith...

You Will Answer My "Prayers".... According To Your Word...

...Finding "Peace" For Your Journey

...For Daily Peace...

Here's

*

A Powerful Word

of

"PEACE"

To Help Me Walk In **"Peace"** ...

Not..."Bitterness & Anger"...

God Will ..."Add"... "Peace"... To My Journey...
"Daily" as I "meditate" on these scriptures of "Peace"

...Finding "Peace" For Your Journey

The ..."Peace of God"...

working in "My Life on ...My "Faith" Journey...

is not determined by what others think or

...believe for me...

it's what I choose to "Meditate On" & "Believe" about the power of God's "Word"...working in and through

me for "myself" ...I must have **"Faith" in God**...

and **"Meditate" on His Word**...daily

in order to **"Trust &"Believe"** He'll do just what ...He said...

in His word....according to (Psalms 29:11)

The Lord will give **"strength"** unto his people;

the Lord will bless his people with **"peace"**...

Today, I choose to trust and believe, that while reading ..."God's Word"...
I'm receiving the "Peace of God" I need to keep me "moving" on My "Faith" Journey

I agree with you_____

according to the "Word of God"... (Matt. 18:19)

...My Journey...

has not always been "FUN" or "Peaceful"... I just recently started calling it a "Faith" Journey. It still amazes me today <u>Thursday May 20th, 2010</u> as I sit and type the words that you're reading "right Now" from a "painful place" on my faith journey. I realize just how powerful the..."Peace of God"... and the ..."Grace of God"... are both at work together providing the "strength" I need ...at 9:45a.m. this morning...to "encourage you" to put your "Trust" in God... while I'm trying to do the same. Want to know a "secret"...I just finished "praying" for one hour and quest what?, my stomach is was hurting and I really didn't "feel" like getting up to pray or to type. <u>But, I'm "trying" to keep my "Commitment" to God</u>

to sit in "His Presences"..."daily" at 8:30a.m.- 9:30a.m. to pray, study, praise, worship and "Hear" from Him what He has prepared for me to do today for Him...even concerning what."He wants" to say to "you" as I type this "little book" for Him. God wants <u>"My Commitment"</u> also, to <u>"MEDITATE On"</u> His

"Word" Daily just a little at a time, as often as I can

This will... help me "write them" on my "Heart & Mind" empowering me to do "spiritual warfare" against the enemy with the... "Word of God" as my weapon and not my flesh when

he comes to "steal my peace". God wants me to ...<u>Commit to confessing them "daily"</u> out loud, no matter how I'm "feeling" that day to help <u>increase my faith in His Word.</u> Do not allow the enemy to "Walk-Out" your "Faith" Journey... with you, robbing your joy daily with "<u>his lies</u>"...causing you to think and confess "Bitterness & Anger" all day long.

Try to "Renew" your mind daily with the ...<u>"Word of God"</u> ... This will empower you to see, think and confess just how

<u>"Blessed & Highly Favored"</u>..you are.

"Adding"... **"Peace"** To Your Journey...

...Is "Easy" For God...

once he can get "you" to truthfully "face" (identify)

the real "Root" of your "Bitterness And Anger" Whenever "Bitterness & Anger" ...shows up on My "Faith" Journey they seem to always have a lot of ..."Questions" ...following them for me to "answer".

Some of them are very important to me and some appear to be very foolish. But, nevertheless the "Word of God" always gives me a "Wisdom Answer" that's "perfect" to help me "Hold My Peace" and remove the "bitterness and anger" that's trying to cause me to "quit" and disagree with

...His Purpose... His Plan...His Will...

for "My Life" and the lives of others "I care" about. Here are a few "daily" questions that will come up on your journey. You'll need to know the "answers" not to be "smarter" than a fifth grader, but to keep the enemy from "destroying" you on your journey.

Be careful "Who" you seek help, advice and answers from when "Bitterness & Anger" is on your path... Remember, Satan was on Jesus path and lead Him into the wilderness to be tempted. But, Jesus was always able to keep His enemy "defeated" with these three words...."It Is Written"

The "Journey of Life" is an "open" book test....
The "Word of God" will help you learn from your mistakes and the mistakes of others if you "read it"... and teach you how to walk in "Righteousness"

On Your ..."Faith"... Journey

...Finding "Peace" For Your Journey

I Pray You'll Soon "Discover" And "Believe"

What Really "Empowers" A Person To

"Keep On Moving"

In Spite of Their Bitterness And Their Anger

Is "Simply" The Way They "Choose"

To "Respond" To The...

Who... What...

When... Where...

Why... How...

"Questions" They Encounter In Life...

On Their "Faith" Journey

Your "Success"... Is Just A "Right" Response Away

From Your "Divine" Destiny

Your "Failure"... Is Just A "Wrong" Response Away

From Your Dark "Defeat"

...Finding "Peace" For Your Journey

Let's Start With A Few **"Simple"** But, Important...

"Questions"

By Answering These "Questions" Correctly

You'll soon See A Very Powerful "Spiritual & Professional" Difference

In Your "Life" And The Lives of Others You Care About...

How We See, Hear, Feel, Understand And Choose

To Handle Our

..."Trials And Tribulations" In Life...

Is What Matters To God... As He Travels "With Us"

On Our "Faith" Journey

"Seeking & Meditating On"
...God's Word... "Daily"

To Find The "Right Answers" To These Simple
"Questions"
Will Soon Give You A Greater **"Peace"**

In Life And Turn Your "Simple" Journey...

...Into A "Faith" Journey...

One That Will "Glorify" God,

Draw Others To Christ,

And Inspire Others To

Seek Thee **"First"** The

... "Kingdom of God" ...

When They "See" The "Power of God"

..."Working In You....

...Finding "Peace" For Your Journey

"First" Set of Questions...

Are To Help You "Understand"

"What"

...You Know And Don't Know About ...

(A Few)

"Spiritual"

...Things...

May This Very ..."Powerful Answer"...

Found In The ...Word Of God...

..."Add Peace"...
To Your "Faith" Journey For Life
*

...Our Spiritual Blessings

...Are In Christ...

(Ephesians 1:2-23)

Grace be to you, and peace,

from God our Father, and from the Lord Jesus Christ.

Blessed be the God and Father of our Lord Jesus Christ, who hath blessed us with all spiritual blessings in heavenly places in Christ.

According as he hath chosen us in him before the foundation of the world, that we should be holy and without blame before him in love:

Having predestinated us unto the adoption of

children by Jesus

Christ to himself, according to the good pleasure of his will.

To the praise of the glory of his grace, wherein he hath made us accepted in the beloved.

In whom we have redemption through his blood, the forgiveness of sins, according to the riches of this grace.

Wherein he hath abounded toward us in all wisdom and prudence;

Having made known unto us the mystery of his will according to his good pleasure which he hath purposed in himself:

That in the dispensation of the fullness of times he might gather together in one all things in Christ, both which are in heaven, and and which are on earth; even in him:

In whom also we have obtained, an inheritance, being predestined according to the purpose of him who worketh all things after the counsel of his own will.

That we should be to the praise of his glory, who first trusted in Christ.

In whom ye also trusted, after that ye heard the word of truth, the gospel of your salvation: in whom also after that ye believed, ye were sealed with the holy Spirit of promise.

Which is the earnest of our inheritance until the redemption of the purchased possession, unto the praise of his glory.

"Pray" Always For Wisdom & Knowledge

Wherefore I also, after I heard of your faith in the Lord Jesus, and love unto all the saints.

Cease not to give thanks for you, making mention of you in my prayers;

That the God of our Lord Jesus Christ, the Father of glory, may give unto you the spirit of wisdom and revelation in the knowledge of him:

The eyes of your understanding being enlightened;

that ye may know what is the hope of his calling and what the riches of the glory of his inheritance in the saints.

And what is the exceeding greatness of his power to us-ward who believe, according to the working of his mighty power,

Which he wrought in Christ, when he raised him from the dead, and set him at his own right hand in the heavenly places.

Far above all principality, and power, and might, and dominion, and every name that is named, not only in this world, but also in that which is to come:

And hath put all things under his feet, and gave him to be the head over all things to the church,

Which is his body, the fullness of him that filleth all.

Anytime Throughout This Book…While Reading
…Any Of These… "Powerful Scriptures" …
…With Understanding…
You Hear, Feel or Sense The Move of The

… "Holy Spirit" …
<u>"Knocking At The Door of Your Heart."</u>

...Finding "Peace" For Your Journey

...Please Do Not Ignore...
The "Lord's Knocking"
Just Stop And "Invite" Him Into Your Heart
...By Faith...
According To His Word... He'll Do the Rest...

(Romans 10:8-13)

But what saith it? The word is nigh thee, even in thy mouth, and in the heart: that is, the word of faith, which we preach.

That if thou shalt confess with thy mouth the Lord Jesus, and shall believe in thine heart that God hath raised him from the dead, thou shalt be saved.

For with the heart man believeth unto righteousness; and with the mouth confession is made unto salvation.

For the scripture saith, Whosoever believeth on him shall not be ashamed. There is no difference between the Jew and the Greek: for the same Lord over all is rich unto all that call upon him. For whosoever shall call upon the name of the Lord shall ne saved.

...Finding "Peace" For Your Journey

He's Adding **"Peace"** To Your Journey...

"Today" With This Powerful **"Question"**

How Well Do You Know...

The "Trinity"

A. God...

B. Jesus...

C. The Holy Spirit...

...Finding "Peace" For Your Journey

*What Does Each One ..."Provide"... For You?

_____

_____

_____

A. God

God... is a "Spirit"

and they that worship him must worship him in spirit and in truth

(John 4:24)

...Finding "Peace" For Your Journey

*What Does ...(John 4:24)... Mean To You?

_____
_____
_____
_____
_____
_____
_____
_____
_____
_____

*Who or What, ...Do You Currently Find Yourself "Worshiping" Instead of God...In Your Life? Why?

_____
_____
_____
_____
_____
_____
_____
_____
_____
_____

I Believe... I Receive... By Faith...

Today I AM_____

...Finding "Peace" For Your Journey

B. Jesus

Looking unto Jesus the author and finisher of our faith; who for the joy that was set before him endured the cross, despising the same, and is set down at the right hand of the throne of God.

(Hebrews 12:2)

...Finding "Peace" For Your Journey

*What Is (Hebrews 12:2) Saying ..."Jesus"... Did For You?

_____
_____
_____
_____
_____

*What Can You Do "Daily" To Be More Like Jesus?

_____
_____
_____
_____
_____
_____
_____
_____

*What Can You Do To..."Introduce"... Others To The Trinity

_____
_____
_____
_____
_____

_____

I Believe... I Receive... By Faith...

Today I CAN_____

...Finding "Peace" For Your Journey

C. The Holy ...Spirit...

But the **"comforter"** which is the **Holy Ghost** "Spirit" whom the Father will send in my name, he shall teach you all things; and bring all things to your remembrance whatsoever I have said unto you.

(John 14:26)

...Finding "Peace" For Your Journey

*What Does "This Word" Mean To You?

_____
_____
_____
_____
_____
_____
_____

*Have You Ever Witnessed The "Power" of The Move of ..."Holy Spirit"... On Others?

_____
_____
_____
_____
_____
_____
_____
_____
_____

I Believe... I Receive... By Faith...

Today I WILL_____

...Finding "Peace" For Your Journey

He's Adding "Peace" To Your Journey

"Today" With This Powerful "Question"

*Who Is "Jesus" To You?

A man name Thomas saith unto him, Lord, we know not whiter thou goest; and how can we know the way? Jesus saith unto him,

I am the way, the truth, and the life:

no man cometh unto the Father, but by me. If ye had known me, ye should have known my father also and from henceforth ye know him and have seen him.　　　　　(John 14:5,6,7)

*List A Few "Names" of God ... That You Know And Share The Meaning.

_____
_____
_____
_____
_____
_____
_____
_____

*When Do You Call On Him ...By These Names?

_____
_____
_____
_____
_____
_____
_____
_____

I Believe... I Receive... By Faith...

Today I NEED_____

...Finding "Peace" For Your Journey

He's Adding "Peace" To Your Journey "Today" With This Powerful "Question"

*Who Is The Holy "Spirit" Ghost...
..To You or A Believer?...

(Acts 1:6,7,8)
When they therefore were come together,

they asked of him, saying, LORD, wilt thou at this time restore again the kingdom to Israel? And he said unto them, It is not for you to know the times of the seasons, which the Father hath put in his own power.

But ye shall **receive power,** after that the **Holy Ghost;** is come upon you: and ye shall be **witnesses unto me** both in Jerusalem, and in all Judaea, and in Samaria, and unto the uttermost part of the earth.

...Finding "Peace" For Your Journey

*What Does He Do For "Believers?" (Read The Book of Acts)

_____
_____
_____
_____
_____

*What Did They "Receive?"

_____
_____
_____
_____

*Do You Have The ..."Holy Ghost?"... Share Your Experience ...the evidence of speaking in tongues?

_____
_____
_____
_____

I Believe... I Receive... By Faith...

Today I WANT_____

...Finding "Peace" For Your Journey

He's Adding **"Peace"** To Your Journey
"Today" With This Powerful **"Question"**

*

*Who Get's To Go To Heaven
For Real?

"A Sinner Saved By Grace"
*

Are You "Saved?"…

Are You A "Believer?"…

Are You A "Born Again" Christian?…

Are You A "Follower" of

…Jesus Christ?…

Or

Just A "Person"... Too Afraid To "Believe In Him"
Waiting For The Enemy To "Trick You"

Out of Your ..."Free" Gift of Salvation?...

Don't "Believe Him" When He Tells You...
Don't Become ...Either One...
And That <u>"No One"</u> Goes To "Heaven or Hell"
...After Death...
Because, There Is No Heaven or Hell

...For Real..

Do You Know A Liar... When You Hear One?

*

What Are Some of Your "True" Thoughts or Beliefs On This "Powerful Question?"

I encourage you to "write out" your thoughts, to strengthen your "confession" of "Faith" because, you'll be surprised how many people you'll meet on your journey... that can not honestly express their "true feelings" about... **"Salvation"**...

The enemy often uses what we don't know or

"believe in" to ...defeat us...

*What Are Some of Your **"True" Thoughts**

...Finding "Peace" For Your Journey

About - Salvation - Heaven - Hell?

_____
_____
_____
_____
_____
_____
_____
_____
_____
_____
_____
_____
_____
_____
_____
_____
_____

I Believe... I Receive... By Faith... I Have

"God's Peace" Today!   In ...His Word... Amen!

...On My Journey...

I do "believe" it's foolish to "live life" not being able to explain to anyone what makes...life worth "living" to you...For the word of God says this,

For none of us liveth to himself, and no man dieth to himself. For whether we live, we live unto the Lord; and whether we die, we die unto the Lord: whether we live therefore, of die, we are the Lord's. For this end Christ both died, and rose, and revived, that he might be Lord both of the dead and living. (Romans 14:7-9)

I encourage you to read the entire chapter about (The weak and the strong) When reading "God's Word" I get so full in my spirit about His Love for me.

When I think about how much God has "SAVED" me from it brings tears to my eyes this morning... July 13th 2010, as God is leading me to come back to this page and "add" this statement for you. As I type and read these powerful words I can feel what

"Apostle Paul" must have being feeling when he wrote... (Philippians 1:16-22)

The one preach Christ of contention, not sincerely, supposing to add affliction to my bonds;

But the other of love, knowing that I am set for the defence of the gospel.

What then? Notwithstanding, every way, whether in pretence, or in truth, Christ is preached; and I therein do rejoice, yea, and will rejoice.

For I know that this shall turn to "my salvation" through your prayer, and the supply of the Spirit of Jesus Christ.

According to my earnest expectation and my hope, that in nothing I shall be ashamed, but that with all boldness, as always, so now also Christ shall be magnified in my body, whether it be by life, or by death.

<u>For to me to live is Christ, and to die is gain.</u>

I have discovered I can't "choose" "salvation" for you or my children. And I'm not smarter than a "fifth grader" who may know all the books in the "Bible".

I'm was proud of my "High School" Diploma and my Cosmetology License. But that was not enough to get me into heaven or hell. I had to "invite" Jesus Christ into my life (my heart) no matter how missed up it was at the time. I had to choose to "believe" He cared enough about me to come and "SAVE ME".

It's only by "Faith" and the "Grace" of God that I'm empowered to write these books for others to read. I just hope and pray that "God" will send someone on your "Proud" Journey soon to lead you to Christ before it's too late. My pride came before my faith and almost killed me. That's why God humbled me to "SAVE ME". Now all I have left is "All In His Hands" for real.

Pride goes before destruction, and an haughty spirit before a fall. Better it is to be of an humble spirit with the lowly than to divide the spoil with the proud

(Proverbs 16:18)

I'm still grateful today that in my early twenties, He sent a beauty older woman in the salon I worked at.

And as I did her make-up I notice a sense of "Peace" in her presence, that I had not experienced since sitting in the "closet" with my grandmother, as a little girl. Now grandma and I would rock, sing and pray to God in that closet for hours having fun, when it rained.

But, now I'm all grown up. And don't attend church as much since grandma has gone home to be with her master. So this "peace" she has now has my attention.

So at first I thought it was because she was white and wealthy. Wrong!.. I asked her to tell me about her "peace" and she shared with me that she was "Born Again"… I remember asking her …what is that?

I knew, but I didn't know it in these words.

Even though I grew up in the "run around" church, you know the one grandma dragged you to on Sunday… The Holy Ghost Church. Once I got there I loved it. I enjoyed beating the one big drum on Sunday with my grandma, as she praised the Lord all day.

I thought it was a "black" religious slave thang. To be "Saved"… from white folks and the devil. I don't remember hearing "born again."

Well I went to her church (Dr. Charles Stanley) the next Sunday and I "invited" ...Jesus... into my life.

this time for ...real... and I became

A "Born Again" ...Christian...

I hope you will "become" one too!

It's the "Best Thing" that ever happen to me.

God always does the drawing... in His Timing...

not just your troubles...

I'm not saying every day of my life has been

..."Peaches and Cream"...

I pray that I'm "Blessed" to "Believe" that I've done what it takes to assure myself, my family

and others that

..."Our Last Walk With Jesus"... Will Lead Us To ...Heaven...On Our "Faith" Journey

God's Timing For Our "Salvation"

Is Always In His ..."Perfect" Timing...

Take A Quick Look At The "Powerful" Conversion of ...Saul...

It will give you a true picture of what God's Grace & Mercy does for You, I, and the body of Christ...

(Acts 9:1-22)

"Apostle Paul"

was known as a very wise man found doing
...foolish things...

He persecuted the Gospel of Jesus Christ, until the Lord "HUMBLED" him by blinding him as he traveled on his "Proud" Journey On Damascus. God lead him blind for three days on a "New Road" ...Straight... by the light of His "Righteousness."

Now look at what he writes in the book of Romans to "help others" understand it's better to become one of these above by "faith" than to die a "blind fool.

(Romans 10:1-4)

BRETHREN, MY heart's desire and prayer to God for Israel is, that they might be saved. For I bear them record that they have a zeal of God, but not according to knowledge.

For the being ignorant of God's righteousness, and going about to establish their own righteousness, have not submitted themselves unto the righteousness of God. For Christ is the end of the law for righteousness to every one the believeth. But what saith it? The word is nigh thee, even in thy mouth, and in thy heart: that is, the word of faith, which we preach.

(Romans 10: 9,10)

That if thou shalt confess wit thy mouth the Lord Jesus, and shalt believe in thine heart that God hath raised him from the dead, thou shalt be saved.

For with the heart man believeth unto righteousness; and with the mouth confession is made unto salvation.

For the scripture saith, Whosoever believeth on him shall not be ashamed. For there is no difference between the Jew and the Greek: for the same Lord over all is rich unto all that call upon him.

For whoever shall call upon the name of the Lord shall be saved.

How then shall they call on him in whom they have not believed? And how shall the believe in him of whom they have not heard: and how shall they hear without a preacher?

And how shall they preach, except they be sent? As it is written, How beautiful are the feet of them that preach the gospel of "peace", and bring glad tidings of good things!

But they have not all obeyed the gospel. For Esaias saith, Lord, who hath believed our report?

So then "faith" cometh by hearing, and hearing by the word of God.

...Finding "Peace" For Your Journey

Day 5

He's Adding **"Peace"** To Your Journey "Today" With This Powerful **"Question"**

*

Who "Baptized" Our Lord Savoir Jesus Christ?

I indeed baptize you with water unto repentance: but he that cometh after me is mightier than I, whose shoes I am not worthy to bear: he shall baptize you with the Holy Ghost; and with fire.

(Matt. 3:11)

*Have You Been …Baptized?...

If so, Write About Your Experience:

_____
_____
_____
_____
_____
_____
_____
_____

***Why Do You "Believe" It Was Needed…
According To The Word of God?**

_____
_____
_____
_____
_____

*Do You Know "Who" Baptized Jesus?

_____
_____
_____

I Believe… I Receive… By Faith…

Today I MUST_____

...Finding "Peace" For Your Journey

He's Adding **"Peace"** To Your Journey "Today" With This Powerful **"Question"**
*

...Which One Are You...
(circle one)

...A Church "Member?"
...A Church "Visitor?"
...A T.V. Church Member?
...A Church Hater?

Why?_____
_____
_____
_____
_____
_____
_____

And having an high priest over the house of God;
Let us draw near with a true heart, in full assurance of faith, having our hearts sprinkled from an evil conscience, and our bodies washed with pure water.
Let us hold fast the profession of our faith without wavering; (for he is faithful that promised;)
And let us consider one another to provoke unto love and to good works:
Not forsaking **"the assembling of ourselves together"** as the manner of some is; but exhorting one another: and so much the more, as you see the day approaching.
For if we "sin willfully" after that we have received the knowledge of the truth; there remaineth no more sacrifice for sins.   (Hebrews 10:21-26)

...Finding "Peace" For Your Journey

*What Do You Believe Is The Difference - Between The Four?

_____
_____
_____
_____
_____

*Why Do You Prefer To Watch Church on T.V.?

_____
_____
_____
_____
_____

*What Do You "Enjoy" The Most About - Going To The Church?

_____
_____
_____
_____
_____

*What Is Your Least "Favorite" Part of Attending Today's Church Services?

_____
_____
_____
_____
_____
_____
_____
_____

*Do You Believe That The "Church" of 'God…

Is In You?

_____
_____
_____
_____
_____
_____
_____
_____

I Believe… I Receive… By Faith… I Have

"God's Peace" Today!   In…His Word…Amen!

Where Does "God" Meet Your
..."Spiritual" Needs...
The Most?

*In His Word?

_____
_____
_____
_____
_____
_____

*In The Church?

_____
_____
_____
_____
_____
_____
_____
_____

...Finding "Peace" For Your Journey

*In The Wisdom of Others?

_____
_____
_____
_____
_____
_____
_____

*In Your Quite Time Alone... Praising Him?

_____
_____
_____
_____
_____
_____

*No Where At All? ... Why Is That?

_____
_____
_____

I Believe... I Receive... By Faith...

Today I AM_____

...Finding "Peace" For Your Journey

He's Adding **"Peace"** To Your Journey
"Today" With This Powerful **"Question"**

Do You ...."Desire"... A Closer

"Relationship" With God?

Like The One "Jesus" Had With His Father "God"

When He Was "Walking-Out" His "Faith" Journey...

Here On Earth?

After reading these verses of scriptures:

*Do you see what kept them "together" to the end of His "Faith" Journey.

_____
_____
_____
_____
_____
_____
_____
_____

*What is really keeping you "together" with the Lord?

_____
_____
_____
_____
_____
_____
_____
_____

I Believe… I Receive… By Faith…

Today I CAN_____

I AM the true vine, and my Father is the husbandman.

Every branch in me that beareth not fruit he taketh away: and every branch that bear fruit, he purgeth it; that it may bring forth more fruit,

Now ye are clean through the word which I have spoken unto you.

Abide in me and I in you, As the branch cannot bear fruit of itself, except ye abide in me;

I am the vine, ye are the branches: He that abideth in me, and I in him, the same bringeth forth much fruit: for without me ye can do nothing.

If a man abide not in me, he is cast forth as a branch, and is withered; and men gather them, and cast them into the fire, and they are burned.

If ye abide in me; and my words abide in you, ye shall ask what ye will, and it shall be done unto you.

Herein is my Father glorified, that ye bear much fruit; so shall ye be my disciples.

As the Father hath loved me, so have I loved you: continue ye in my love.

If ye Keep my commandments, ye shall abide in my love; even as I have kept my Father's commandments, and abide in his love.

These things have I spoken unto, that my joy might remain in you, and that your joy might be full.

This is my commandment, That you love one another, as I have loved you.

Greater love hath no man than this, that a man lay down his life for for his friends. You are my friends, if ye do whatsoever I command you.

...Finding "Peace" For Your Journey

"Second" Set of Questions...

Are To Help You "Discover"

"Where"

You Are... On Your Journey...

"Spiritually"

Are You "Walking" In The **"Spirit"**

Or Walking In The **"Flesh?"**

...Finding "Peace" For Your Journey

...Not Sure?...

✶

May This Very ..."Powerful Answer"...

Found In The ...Word Of God...

..."Add Peace"...
To Your "Faith" Journey For Life
✶

...Fulfilling The Law of Christ...

(Galatians 5:24-25)

And they that are Christ's have crucified the flesh with the affections and lusts. If We live in the Spirit, let us also walk in the Spirit.

..."Liberty"... Defined

(Galatians 5: 13-18)

For, brethren, ye have been called unto liberty; only use not liberty; only use not liberty for an occasion to the flesh, but by love serve one another.

For all the law is fulfilled in one word, even in this;

Thou shalt love thy neighbor as thyself.

But if ye bite and devour one another.

This I say then "Walk In The Spirit" and ye shall not fulfill the lust of the flesh.

For the flesh lusteth against the Spirit, and the Spirit against the flesh; and these are contrary the one to the other: so that ye cannot do the things that ye would.

But if ye be led of the Spirit, ye are not under the law.

...Finding "Peace" For Your Journey

Day 8

He's Adding "Peace" To Your Journey

"Today" With This Powerful "Question"

*

What Do You "Believe"
...God... Can Do To
Change Your "Situation?"

... "Meditate On" This Scripture...

(Haggai 2:9)

The glory of this latter house shall be greater than of the former, saith the LORD of hosts: and in this place will I give "PEACE" saith the LORD of hosts.

...Finding "Peace" For Your Journey

*This Morning_____

What Things Does "His Word" Say - He Will Do For You?

_____
_____
_____
_____
_____
_____

*This Afternoon_____

What Makes You "Believe"...He Will Do Them?..."Be Honest"

_____
_____
_____
_____
_____
_____
_____

*This Evening_____

"Ask Him" What "Changes" You Need Making Today

_____
_____
_____
_____
_____
_____
_____

I Believe... I Receive... By Faith...

Today I WILL_____

...Finding "Peace" For Your Journey

Day 9

He's Adding "Peace" To Your Journey

"Today" With This Powerful "Question"

Did You ..."Lose It"...
The "Fear" of The LORD?

..."Meditate On" This Scripture...

(Malachi 2:6)

My covenant was with him of life and "Peace" and I gave them to him for the fear wherewith he feared me, and was afraid before my name.

The law of truth was in his mouth, and iniquity was not found in his lips: he walked with me in "Peace"

and equity, and did turn many away from iniquity.

For the "Priest's" lips should keep knowledge, and they should seek the law at his mouth: for he is the messenger of the LORD of hosts.

...Finding "Peace" For Your Journey

***This Morning...** What are you afraid of more than "God?"

_____
_____
_____
_____
_____
_____

***This Afternoon...** Find scriptures to remove that fear

_____
_____
_____
_____
_____
_____

***This Evening...** Confess it! Give it to the Lord in "Prayer"

_____
_____
_____
_____
_____
_____
_____

I Believe... I Receive... By Faith...

Today I NEED _____

...Finding "Peace" For Your Journey

He's Adding **"Peace"** To Your Journey

"Today" With This Powerful **"Question"**

*

Are You Willing To "Fast & Pray?"

..."Meditate On" This Scripture...

(Zechariah 8:19)

Thus saith the LORD of hosts; The fast of the fourth month, and the fast of the fifth, and the fast of the seventh, and the fast of the tenth, shall be to the house of Judah joy and gladness, and cheerful feasts; therefore love the truth and "Peace" Thus saith the LORD of hosts; *It shall yet come to pass,* that there shall come people, and the inhabitants of many cities:

And the inhabitants of one city shall go to another, saying, Let us go speedily to pray before the LORD, and to seek the LORD of hosts: I will go also.

...Finding "Peace" For Your Journey

*What Are You Willing To ..."Give Up" ...To Get What You Are Believing God To Do For You On Your "Faith" Journey?

*This Morning...

_____
_____
_____
_____
_____
_____

*This Afternoon...

_____
_____
_____
_____
_____

*This Evening...

_____
_____
_____
_____

I Believe... I Receive... By Faith...

Today I WANT_____

...Finding "Peace" For Your Journey

He's Adding **"Peace"** To Your Journey Today
*What's On Your Mind?

_____
_____

Do You ..."Trust" ...The Lord

With "Every" Thing In Your Life?

_____

..."Meditate On" This Scripture...

(Proverbs 3:5,6)

<u>Trust</u> in the LORD with all thine heart; and <u>lean not</u> unto thine own understandingl In all thy ways <u>acknowledge him,</u> and he shall direct thy path.

*Tell the LORD…why you "struggle" with doing these …"three things"…sometimes

*Trust

_____
_____
_____
_____
_____
_____
_____

*Lean Not

_____
_____
_____
_____

*Acknowledge Him

_____
_____
_____
_____
_____
_____

I Believe… I Receive… By Faith…

Today I MUST_____

...Finding "Peace" For Your Journey

He's Adding "Peace" To My Journey Today
*What's On Your Mind?

_____
_____
_____

Has He Been "Faithful" To You?

..."Meditate On" This Scripture...

(1 Corinthians 1:9)

And He will establish you to the end (keep you steadfast, give you strength, and guarantee your vindication; He will be your warrant against all accusation or indictment so that you will be) quiltless and irreproachable in the day of our Lord Jesus Christ (the Messiah)

God is faithful (reliable, trustworthy, and therefore ever true to His promise; and He can be depended on); by Him you were called into companionship and participation with His Son, Jesus Christ our Lord.

...Finding "Peace" For Your Journey

How Has "God" Been
..."Faithful To You... On Your Journey, So far?

_____

_____

_____

_____

_____

_____

_____

_____

_____

_____

_____

_____

_____

_____

I Believe... I Receive... By Faith...

My God IS_____

...Take A Moment And Think...
Do you know the "spiritual meaning" of these "Powerful Words?"

...Faith...
...Faithful...
...Faithfulness...

and

...This Powerful Statement...

For We Walk By ..."Faith"...

(we regulate our lives and conduct ourselves by our conviction or belief respecting man's relationship to God and divine things, with trust and holy fervor; thus we walk) not by sight or appearance.

(Yes) we have confident and hopeful courage and are pleased rather to be away from home out of the body and be at home with the Lord.

(2 Corinthians 5:7-8) amplified

I would love to type the …"Whole Bible"…

for you, but I can't.

There is so much a "Believer" needs to learn about "FAITH."

But, most importantly you need to know that

…"FAITH"… worketh by …LOVE…

and that without "FAITH" it's impossible to

"Please God."

Now take a moment and read this entire "powerful chapter" and decide if you know enough about "FAITH" to confess to yourself and others…you are…

traveling on a …"FAITH" Journey… with God.

If not, immediately find you a dictionary and look up these "powerful words" and write out the "real definition" to give you a better "understanding" so you can decide if you want to continue walking out a very "dangerous journey" with the enemy..or stop and "Invite Jesus" into your life and start your

…"FAITH" …Journey with God…

…"IMMEDIATELY"…Today! By FAITH.

Now "FAITH" is the substance of things hoped for, the evidence of things not seen.

(Hebrew 11:1)

Know therefore that the LORD thy God, he is God, the <u>"Faithful"</u> God, which keepeth covenant and mercy with them that love him and keep his commandments to thousand generations;

(Deuteronomy 7:9)

HEAR MY prayer, O LORD, give ear to my supplications: in thy <u>"Faithfulness"</u> answer me, and in thy righteousness.

(Psalms 143: 1)

So then <u>"Faith"</u> cometh by hearing, and hearing by the word of God.

(Romans 10:17)

But Without <u>"Faith"</u> it is impossible to please him: for he that cometh to God must believe that he is, and that he is a rewarder of them that diligently seek him.

(Hebrews 11:6)

Take A Moment
...And Write Down...

a brief "confession of your heart" that will

"Add Peace" to your journey today by using

...these powerful words...

...Faith......Faithful......Faithfulness

_____
_____
_____
_____
_____
_____
_____
_____
_____
_____
_____
_____

...Finding "Peace" For Your Journey

He's Adding "Peace" To Your Journey Today
*What's On Your Mind?

___

Have You Been ..."Faithful"...
To God And Others...On Your Journey?

..."Meditate On" This Scripture...
(Luke 16:10-13)

He that is "faithful" in that which is least is "faithful" also in much: and he that is unjust in the least is unjust also in much.
If therefore ye have not been faithful in the unrighteous mammon, who will commit to your trust the true riches?
And if ye have not been faithful in that which is another's man's, who shall give you that which is your own?
No servant can serve two masters: for either he will hate the one, and love the other; or else he will hold to the one, and despise the other. Ye cannot serve
...God and mammon....

...Finding "Peace" For Your Journey

*In The Mornings ...What Do You Do To Get Closer To God?

_____
_____
_____
_____
_____
_____

*In The Afternoons.... How Can You "Serve" God?

_____
_____
_____
_____
_____
_____
_____
_____
_____

*In The Evenings... How Can You Show Your "Appreciation?'

_____
_____
_____
_____
_____
_____
_____

I Believe... I Receive... By Faith...

My God HAS_____

...Finding "Peace" For Your Journey

...On My Journey...

Seems "Bitterness & Anger"

shows up the most

when things go wrong when "faithfulness" is missing by others I'm depending on for help.

I found it's not about their "faithfulness" to me, but my "faithfulness" to God that gives me peace and his "faithfulness" to me. Even when I'm not faithful all the time... **He Is!**

Do You Remember How "Faithful" He Was To

...Abraham & Sarah?...

What did he promise to give them?_____

Be Careful!

The enemy loves to remind us when we come up short, not being faithful to God.
Stop and find the scripture that tells you
All Have **"Sinned"** And Come
"Short" of The "Glory" of God

...Finding "Peace" For Your Journey

... Do You Know ...

what PAIN or who causes you to stop being
"Faithful" God and others you care about?

Be ..."Honest"... With Yourself About Your

Pressures...Addictions...Insecurities...Needs

_____
_____
_____
_____
_____
_____
_____
_____
_____
_____
_____
_____
_____
_____

I Believe... I Receive... By Faith...

My God NEVER_____

...Finding "Peace" For Your Journey

He's Adding "Peace" To Your Journey Today
*What's On Your Mind?

_____
_____
_____

Does Your "Family" Know How Much You ...Love God?...

..."Meditate On" This Scripture...

(1 Corinthians 13:1-3)
THOUGH I speak with the tongues of men and of angels, and have not charity, (LOVE) I am become as sounding brass, or a tinkling cymbal.
And though I have the gift of prophecy, and understanding all mysteries, and all knowledge; and though I have all faith, so that I could remove mountains, and have not charity, (LOVE)
I am nothing.
And though I bestow all my goods to feed the poor, and though I give my body to be burned, and have not charity, it profiteth me nothing

...Finding "Peace" For Your Journey

...Loving Yourself And Others...

The "Wrong" Way

Will Cause You Great ..."PAIN"...
Pressure... Addictions... Insecurities...Needs...
...On Your "Faith" Journey...

That's why you will need to take the **"Agape"**
..."LOVE Test"... often on your Journey.

Many times you will be tempted to let your "fleshly mind" handle your bitterness and anger towards others, rather than let the "Agape Love" constrain you from willing looking forward to getting revenge.

...The "God – Kind" of Love Forgives

One characteristic of the "Agape Love" is that it "forgives." When God's love is in demonstration, there is a "attitude of forgiveness" because love and forgiveness go hand and hand.

(Ephesians 4:32)

And be ye "kind" one to another, tenderhearted, forgiving one another, even as God for Christ's sake hath "forgiven" you.

(1 Corinthians 13:4-8)

Charity suffereth long, and is kind;
charity envieth not; charity vaunteth not itself, is not puffed up.
Doth not behave itself unseemly,
seeketh not her own, is not easily provoked, thinketh no evil;
Rejoiceth not in iniquity,
but rejoiceth in the truth; Beareth all things, endureth all things.
Charity never faileth:
but whether there be prophecies, they shall fail; whether there be tongues, they shall cease; whether there be knowledge, it shall vanish away.

What Does …(1 John 4:7-12)… Instruct You To Do?

That…"Worldly Love"…Does Not?

_____
_____
_____
_____
_____
_____

...Finding "Peace" For Your Journey

...Agape Love Test...

*What Did "God" Do To "Show His "Agape Love" To You?

_____
_____
_____
_____

*How Do You "Share" Your "Agape Love" With Others?

_____
_____
_____
_____

*Who Do You Need To..."Forgive"... And Show Agape Love?

_____
_____
_____
_____

*Where Do You "Search" For Love?

_____
_____
_____
_____

I Believe... I Receive... By Faith...

My God DID_____

...Finding "Peace" For Your Journey

"Third" Set of Questions...

Are To Help You "Identify"

Your ..."Traveling"... Companions

"Who"

Are You ..."Waking With"... Most of The Time

On Your "Faith" Journey?

"Joy & Peace"... "Grace & Glory"

Or

..."Bitterness & Anger"...

..."Suffering & Sorrow"...

May This Very ..."Powerful Answer"...

Found In The ...Word Of God...

..."Add Peace"...
To Your "Faith" Journey For Life
*

...Our Spiritual Companion's...

Advice Should "Always" Keep Us On The "Path" of

...Righteousness...

And Encourage Us To Put Our Total

"Trust" ...In God & His Word...

(Proverbs 13:20)

He that walketh with wise men shall be wise: but a companion of fools shall be destroyed.

Unto you, O men, I call; and my voice is to the sons of man.

O ye simple, understand wisdom: and, ye fools be ye of an understanding heart. Hear; for I will speak of excellent things; and the opening of my lips shall be right things.

For my mouth shall speak truth; and wickedness; there is nothing forward or perverse in them. They are all plain to him that understandeth, and right to them that find knowledge.

Receive my instruction, and not silver; and knowledge rather than choice gold.

For wisdom is better that rubies; and all the things that may be desired are not to be compared to it.

I wisdom dwell with prudence, and find out knowledge of witty inventions.

The fear of the LORD is to hate evil: pride, and arrogancy, and the evil way, and the forward mouth, do I hate.

Counsel is mine, and sound wisdom: I am understanding; I have strength.

...Finding "Peace" For Your Journey

Day 15

He's Adding **"Peace"** To Your Journey Today
"Today" With... **"His Word"**

*

When You're Feeling ..."Lost" ...
...On Your Journey...

Which of Your "Companions" Guides You
"Safely" Back On The ..."Right Path"...
Joy, Peace, Bitterness, Anger, Suffering, Sorrow or
Mercy, Grace & Glory?

..."Meditate On" This Scripture...

(Proverbs 13:20)
He that walketh with wise men shall be wise: but a companion of fools shall be destroyed.

...Finding "Peace" For Your Journey

List A Few ... "Wise People" ...
God Is Using ...To Help You... Keep Pressing On ...On Your Faith Journey...

*When "Bitterness & Anger" Shows Up To Stop You!

_____
_____
_____
_____
_____

*Why Do You Trust Their "Wisdom?"

_____
_____
_____
_____
_____

*Do You "Feel" You're On The "Right Path" Now? ....or Lost?...

_____
_____
_____

I Believe... I Receive... By Faith...

My God WAS_____

...Finding "Peace" For Your Journey

Day 16

**He's Adding "Peace" To Your Journey
"Today" With... "His Word"**

*

**When You Are Feeling
..."Confused or Fearful"...**

"Bitter & Angry" ...About Having To Make
"Life Changing" Decisions
Who Do You "Trust" To Seek Wise Council From?...

..."Meditate On" This Scripture...

(Proverbs 13:1)

A WISE son
heareth his father's instruction: but a scorner heareth not rebuke.

...Finding "Peace" For Your Journey

*How Often Do You Put "Your Trust" In God?
_____
_____
_____
_____

*Who's Currently A Spiritual "Father or Mother" In Your Life?
_____
_____
_____
_____

*Why Do You "Trust" Their Wisdom?
_____
_____
_____
_____

*What Are You "Confused or Fearful" of Right Now?
_____
_____
_____
_____

I Believe... I Receive... By Faith...
My God SEES_____

...On My Journey...

There are times when the more "I think" about all the decisions I have to make just to "keep moving" and not quit, I often get angry with others and God. It's hard to trust others for their wisdom when you're not in the "right spirit", meaning you feel it's your final decision, no matter what the outcome is, so why ask them. Well that's true however, I've found the "Word of God" to always have a "Wisdom Answer" for my every concern.

I try to always seek Godly council from the bible and spiritual friends. But, then the "spirit of pride" comes and tells me I should not ask or seek help from others until I've tried it my way first. "WRONG"... My own "choices" can get me in worst trouble than others if I don't learn to put my total trust in... God and His Word to advise me, comfort me, teach me and guide me for life on... "My Faith Journey"

...Finding "Peace" For Your Journey

...Here's Why...

Take A Close Look At These Powerful Scriptures In (Proverbs 14)

<u>EVERY WISE</u> woman buildeth her house: but the foolish plucketh it down with her hands. (v1)

(I actually did this one for real) ... I broke up my happy home & family

In the mouth of the foolish is a rod of pride: but the lips of the wise shall preserve them. (v3)

A scorner seeketh wisdom, and findeth it not: but knowledge is easy unto him that understandeth. (v6)

Go from the presence of a foolish man, when thou perceives not in him the lips of knowledge. (v 7)

The heart knoweth his own bitterness, and a stranger doth not intermeddle with his joy. (v10)

There is a way which seemeth right unto a man, but the end thereof are the ways of death. (v12)

...Finding "Peace" For Your Journey

He's Adding **"Peace"** To Your Journey

"Today" With... **"His Word"**

*

When You Are **"Feeling The Need"** To Make ..."**Unrighteous**"... Decisions ...

To Keep "Joy & Peace" With Others

..."Meditate On" This Scripture...
(Proverbs 13:6)

Righteousness keepeth him that is upright in the way: but wickedness overthroweth the sinner.

...Finding "Peace" For Your Journey

*Who's Really To Blame For Your Choices?

_____
_____
_____
_____
_____
_____

*How Do You Experience The "Joy & Peace" of God?

_____
_____
_____
_____
_____
_____

*Is It Really Worth It In The End?

_____
_____
_____
_____
_____
_____

I Believe... I Receive... By Faith...

My God MUST_____

...Finding "Peace" For Your Journey

He's Adding **"Peace"** To Your Journey

"Today" With... **"His Word"**

*

When You're Feeling ..."Lonely"...
Does..."Suffering & Sorrow" ...

Comfort You With ...Truth or Lies?

..."Meditate On" This Scripture...

(Psalms 120:1-7)

IN MY distress I cried unto the LORD,

and he heard me.

Deliver my soul, O LORD, from lying lips, and from a deceitful tongue. What shall be given unto thee? Or what shall be done unto thee, thou false tongue?

Sharp arrows of the mighty, with coals of juniper;

Woe is me, that I sojourn in Mesech, that I dwell in the tents of Kedar! My soul hath long dwelt with him that hateth peace. I am for peace: but when I speak, they are for war.

Who Have You Made Your "Life Coach" …Instead of God?…

Do They Know God's Plans For "Your Life?"…
If so, …Do You Agree?… Write What You Know..

_____
_____
_____
_____
_____
_____
_____
_____
_____
_____

I Believe… I Receive… By Faith… I Have "God's Peace" Today!   In…His Word…Amen!

...Finding "Peace" For Your Journey

He's Adding **"Peace"** To Your Journey

"Today" With... **"His Word"**

*

When You Are Feeling

...**"Bitter & Angry"**...
about
Your **"Faith"** Journey

Where Do You Find "Relief?"

*In The
Morning_____

Be ye angry, and sin not: let not the sun go
down upon your wrath
(Ephesians 4:26)

...Finding "Peace" For Your Journey

*In The
Afternoon_____

But now ye also put off all these; anger, wrath, malice, blasphemy, filthy communication out of your mouth

(Colossians 3:8)

*In The
Evening_____

Let all bitterness, and wrath, and anger, and clamour, and evil speaking, be put away from you, with malice:

(Ephesians 4:31)

...In The Word of God or With Others?...
Why? Quickly Read... (Proverbs 13:13)

_____
_____
_____
_____
_____
_____

I Believe... I Receive... By Faith...

Today I AM_____

...Finding "Peace" For Your Journey

He's Adding **"Peace"** To Your Journey
"Today" With..."**His Word**"

When You're Feeling
The ..."**Joy & Peace**"... of "Good Times"...
Who Do You "Them" Celebrate With?

..."Meditate On" This Scripture...
(Matthew 10:12-14)

And when you come into the house, salute it. And if the house be worthy, let **your peace** come upon it: but if it be not worthy, let your peace return to you. And whosoever shall not receive you, nor hear your words, when ye depart out of that house or city, shake off the dust of your feet.

...God's "Blessings"...
Are Often Used The ..."Wrong Way"...
We "Celebrate" Them With The "Wrong People"

*

Who or What... Is Robbing God's ..."Blessings"...

From You...On Your "Faith" Journey?... How – Why?

_____
_____
_____
_____
_____
_____
_____
_____
_____
_____
_____
_____
_____
_____
_____

I Believe... I Receive... By Faith...

My God CAN_____

...Finding "Peace" For Your Journey

He's Adding **"Peace"** To Your Journey

"Today" With... **"His Word"**

*

When Your "Heart" Is Feeling

..."Broken"...

Who Repairs It?

_____
_____
_____

..."Meditate On" This Scripture...

(Luke 4:18)

The ...**Spirit**... of the Lord is upon me,

because he hath anointed me to preach the gospel to the poor; he hath sent me to heal the brokenhearted, to preach deliverance to the captives, and recovering of sight to the blind, to set at liberty them that are bruised.

...Finding "Peace" For Your Journey

*This Morning_____

Tell God What You "Believe" Is Breaking Your "Heart"

LET NOT your heart be troubled; ye believe in God, believe also in me.

(John 14:1)

*This Afternoon_____

Ask God To Show You What He Sees In Your "Heart"

Search me, O God, and know my heart: try me, and. Now my thoughts: And see if there be any wicked way in me, and lead me in the way everlasting   (Psalms 139:23,24)

*This Evening_____

Pray The "Spirit of The Lord" To Come Upon You

Hope deferred maketh the heart sick: but when the desire cometh is is a tree of life.

(Proverbs 13:12)

...Finding "Peace" For Your Journey

"Forth" Set of Questions Are To Help You ..."Remember"...

"When"

God...Showed Up ... On Your Journey

And **"Blessed"** You Real Good...

In Spite of Your "Bitterness & Anger"

May This Very ..."Powerful Answer"...

Found In The ...Word Of God...

... "Add Peace"...

To Your ..."Faith" Journey... For Life

...Finding "Peace" For Your Journey

Do You ..."Believe"...

God's

...Grace & Mercy...

...Will Always Get The Job Done...

...Anytime & Anywhere?...

(2 Corinthians 9:8)

And God is able to make all grace abound toward you; that ye, always having all sufficiency in all things may abound to every good work.

...Finding "Peace" For Your Journey

If, so then ... "Always"...

God Has A Safe Place

For All "Believers" To Go To Get The "Help They Need"

(Hebrews 4:16)

Let us then fearlessly and confidently and boldly draw near to the

...Throne of Grace...

(the throne of God's unmerited favor to us sinners), that we may receive mercy (for our failures) and find grace to help in good time for every need (appropriate help and well-timed help, coming just when we need it).

...Finding "Peace" For Your Journey

When "Trouble" Comes
...Your Way...

- Who Is The "First Person"... You Call On?...
- Who Is The Only Person You Expect...
  ...To Come "Help You"...

No Matter What Type of "Trouble" You Are In?...

I Can Always "Remember"
Hearing "Old Folks"
...Confessing These "Powerful Scriptures"...

With So Much "Confidence"

When "Trouble Times" Came Their Way...

I will lift up mine eyes unto the hills, from whence cometh my help. <u>My help cometh from the LORD,</u> which made heaven and earth. He will not suffer thy foot to be moved: he that keepeth thee will not slumber; Behold, he that

...Finding "Peace" For Your Journey

keepeth Israel shall neither slumber nor sleep. The LORD is thy keeper: the LORD is thy shade upon thy right hand.

The sun shall not smite thee by, nor the moon by night. The LORD shall preserve thee from all evil: he shall preserve thy soul.

The LORD shall preserve thy going out and thy coming in from this time forth, and even for evermore.

(Psalms 121:1-8)

For in the time of trouble he shall hide me in his pavilion: in the secret of his tabernacle shall he hide me; he shall set me up upon a rock.

(Psalms 27:5)

*Who else can you "call for help" in times of trouble?

_____
_____
_____
_____
_____
_____

I Believe... I Receive... By Faith...

My God WILL_____

...Finding "Peace" For Your Journey

Do You "Remember"

Just A ..."Few Times"... When You Where In

..."Great Trouble"...

And The "Lord God"

..."Showed Up & Showed Out"...

"For You" ......When "Others" .....Didn't Think You "Deserved" Help?

(list a few trials & victories)

_____

_____

_____

_____

_____

_____

_____

_____

_____

_____

_____

...Finding "Peace" For Your Journey

Why Do You Think He

..."Did It"...

So Many Times?

According ...To "His Word"... (Joshua 1:5-7)

(list a few of the "promise" scriptures ...written on your heart)

_____
_____
_____
_____
_____
_____
_____
_____
_____
_____
_____
_____
_____

...Finding "Peace" For Your Journey

He's Adding **"Peace"** To Your Journey

"Today" With

His Mighty Acts of ..."Power"...
...He Did It For Them!...

Spoke "PEACE" ...To Their Storm...

✶

(Luke 8:22-25) amplified

One of those days He and His disciples got into a boat, and He said to them, Let us go across to the other side of the lake. So they put out to sea.

But as they were sailing, He fell off to sleep. And a whirlwind revolving from below upwards swept down on the lake, and the boat was filling with water, and they were in great danger.

And the disciples came and woke Him, saying, Master, Master, we are perishing! And He, being thoroughly awakened, censured and blamed and rebuked the wind and the raging waves; and they ceased, and there came a calm.

And He said to them, (Why are you so fearful?) Where is your faith? (your trust, your confidence in Me_in My veracity and My integrity)? And they were seized with alarm and profound and reverent dread, and they marveled, saying to one another, Who then is this that He commands even wind and sea, and they obey Him?

Thank God ... He Added "Peace"
...To Their Journey...

...Finding "Peace" For Your Journey

Day 23

He's Adding **"Peace"** To Your Journey

"Today" With

His Mighty Acts of ..."Authority"...
...He Did It For Them!...

Cast Out The ...Unclean Spirit...

*

(Mark 1:21-28) amplified

And they entered into Capernaum, and immediately on the Sabbath He went into the synagogue and began to teach. And they were completely astonished at His teaching for He was teaching as one who possessed authority, and not as the scribes.

Just at that time there was in their synagogue a man (who was in the power) of an unclean spirit; and now (immediately) he raised a deep and terrible cry from the depths of his throat, saying what have you to do

...Finding "Peace" For Your Journey

with us, Jesus of Nazareth?
Have you come to destroy us?
I know who you are -the Holy One of God!
And Jesus rebuked him, saying, hush up
(be muzzled, gagged).
And come out of him! And the unclean spirit,
throwing the man into convulsions and screeching
with a loud voice came out of him.
And they were all so amazed and almost terrified that
they kept questioning and demanding one of another,
saying What is this? What new (fresh) teaching!
With authority He give orders even to the
unclean spirits and they obey Him!
And immediately rumors concerning Him spread
(everywhere) throughout all the region
surrounding Galilee.

*
Thank God ... He Added "Peace" ...To His Journey...

...Finding "Peace" For Your Journey

He's Adding **"Peace"** To Your Journey

"Today" With

His Mighty Acts of ..."Justice"...

...He Did It For Them!...
The Widow And ...The Judge...
*

(Luke 18:1-8) amplified

Also (Jesus) told them a parable to the effect that they ought always to pray and not to turn coward (faint, lose heart, and give up). He said, In a certain city there was a judge who neither reverenced and feared God nor respected or considered man.

And there was a widow in the city who kept coming to him and saying, Protect and defend and give me justice against my adversary.

And for a time he would not; but later he said to himself, Though I have neither reverence or fear for God nor respect or consideration for man.

Yet because this widow continues to bother me,
I will defend and protect and avenge her, lest she give me intolerable annoyance and wear me out by her continual coming or at the last she come and rail on me or assault me or strangle me. Then the Lord said, Listen to what the unjust judge says! And will not (our just) God defend and protect and avenge His elect (His chosen ones), who cry Him day and night? Will He defer them and delay help on their behalf? I tell you, He will defend and protect and avenge them speedily. However, when the Son of Man comes, will He find (persistence in) faith on the earth?

Thank God ... He Added "Peace" ...To Her Journey...

...Finding "Peace" For Your Journey

Do You "Remember"
When... "God"... Gave You "Justice"
Against Your Adversary?

_____

_____

_____

_____

_____

_____

_____

_____

_____

_____

_____

_____

_____

I Have "God's Peace" Today!

Because of The "Great Things" He's Doing For Me

...On My "Faith" Journey...

...Finding "Peace" For Your Journey

He's Adding **"Peace"** To My Journey "Today" With

His Might Acts of ..."Healing"...
...He Did It For Them!...
Healed The Ten ...Lepers...

*

(Luke 17:11-19) amplified

As He went on His way to Jerusalem, it occurred that (Jesus) was passing (along the border) between Samaria and Galilee. And as He was going into one village, He was met by ten lepers,
who stood at a distance.
And they raised up their voices and called, Jesus, Master, take pity and have mercy on us! And when He saw them, He said to them, Go (at once) and show yourselves to the priests, And as they went, they were

cured and made clean, Then one of them, upon seeing that he was cured, turned back, recognizing ad thanking and praising God with a loud voice:
And he fell prostrate at Jesus' feet, thanking Him (over and over). And he was a Samaritan.
Then Jesus asked, Were not (all) ten cleansed? Where are the nine? Was there no one found to return and to recognize give thanks and praise to God except this alien? And He said to him, Get up and go on your way. Your faith (your trust and confidence that spring from your belief in God) has restored you to health.
...What "touches you" most about this story...
The 10 Healing Miracles of Jesus or
The One Grateful Heart of A Sinner?

_____
_____
_____

*
Thank God ... He Added "Peace" ...To Their Journey...

...Finding "Peace" For Your Journey

Do You "Remember"
When..."God"...Performed "A Miracle" For You And Others?

_____
_____
_____
_____
_____
_____
_____
_____
_____
_____
_____
_____
_____
_____

I Have "God's Peace" Today!

Because of The "Great Things" He's Doing For Me

...On My "Faith" Journey...

...Finding "Peace" For Your Journey

How Did You ..."Show"... God
You're Gratitude?

_____
_____
_____
_____
_____
_____
_____
_____
_____
_____
_____
_____
_____
_____
_____
_____

I Have "God's Peace" Today!

Because Of The "Great Things" He's Doing For Me

...On My "Faith" Journey...

...Finding "Peace" For Your Journey

He's Adding **"Peace"** To Your Journey "Today" With

His Mighty Acts of ..."Forgiveness"...
...He Did It For Him!...

Forgave & Restored ...The lost Son...

*

(Luke 15:11-24)

And he said, A certain man had two sons; And the younger of them said to his father, Father give me the portion of goods that falleth to me.

And he divided unto them his living. And not many days after the younger son gathered all together, and took his journey into a far country, and there wasted his substance with riotous living.
And when he had spent all, there arose a mighty famine in that land; and he began to be in want.
And he went and joined himself to a citizen of that

country; and he sent him into his fields to fee swine.

And he would fain have filled his belly with the husks that the swine did eat: and no man gave unto him.

<u>And when he came to himself,</u> he said, How many hired servants of my father's have bread enough and to spare, and I perish with hunger!

I will arise and go to my father, and will say unto him, Father, I have sinned against heaven, and before thee.

And no more worthy to be called thy son; make me as one of thy hired servants. And he rose, and came to his father,

But when he was yet a great way off, his father say him, and had compassion, and ran, and fell on his neck, and kissed him.

Thank God ... He Added "Peace" ...To His Journey...

...Finding "Peace" For Your Journey

...On My Journey...

When I read this story or hear this story preached about from the word of God, about the "good and bad" decisions the "Prodigal Son" made on his "Proud Journey" to destruction, it still brings tears to my eyes. Even on today July 26, 2010 at 1:52p.m., I can remember when his story became so much like my true story when it happened to me for real. God was giving me a "WARNING" then.

I'll tell you about the "second" time I was faced with this "life changing" experience. It was after the death of my brother Danny. He passed February 3rd, 1989, and I was in a backsliding state of mind to say the least. I turned to drugs and drinking daily instead of turning to the LORD ...

Each day I got up very bitter and angry, because he was gone for good, and I loved him dearly, I still needed him "badly" even sick with aids in my missed up life to "fix it" like he's always done for me in the past, because he was always "strong" and he loved me enough to carry my burdens and my pains. The Lord had given me a word of knowledge about him having aids back on Christmas of 1987 before it was for sure.

He was so handsome, "Butch" talented and lovable by many women to be gay. That's what made me "angry and bitter." His Choice to be gay and to stay gay! He told me why he could not stay with the women. He didn't want to affect them or his family if he didn't stay "faithful." He had a few girlfriends throughout high school and other times. They loved him dearly.

My mother loved him unconditionally all her life, but we all had "deadly issues" that required so much love just to keep us alive. We love hard from a sick place I see now. Maybe that's why my mother blessed me and other family members and friends abundantly with the insurance money. Because I know the pain of why we even had this money in the first, I was more than grateful to receive it.

So I held on to that money tight, by the Grace of God, even though I got high daily for about seven good months until the Lord personally delivered me from it all in September 1989. I re-dedicated my life to Christ and never went to Rehab.

I was sold out till, the year July 1994. Then I was back selling cars and rolling. I felt in this season I was "anointed to prosper" and had the wisdom to be a good steward over all my money, including my "in heritage" and my son's too.

By know you should know where this "short true story" is headed. Does it sound like one of yours?

I "saved" ten thousand dollars my first year from just bonus money, while selling cars. Then I made it to the big leagues "mortgage" business by July, 1998 still rolling. By Dec. 1998, I "earned" my first ten thousand that month. I continued to earn seven to eight thousand dollars a month for a few months straight.

By now I was known as A PROUD "BAD SISTA." Bold-Anointed-Determined. It was if God was giving me all the things I ask for in life, things I had only dreamed of ever having for real and then some, two Mercedes, a convertible, built a five bedroom new home, clothes, jewelry, Gold American EXP. (smile) don't laugh I was proud of getting these things finally.

Remember I came from the projects and dreaming of a white Christmas was not "my dream". I dreamed of living like "WHITE" people and having everything. So when the Blessings of the Lord and Satan showed up and "Blessed Me Real Good" and over took me, I couldn't "discern" between the two. I was living the "Good Life" – I thought it was truly the "God-Life."

I was just happy to be black and "Project Rich" (money and no wisdom) or Church Rich - "Blessed &

...Finding "Peace" For Your Journey

Highly Favored" by God we say... taking a short break from "robbing-Peter to pay-Paul" for a little while. After being "drug free" for eleven years...the enemy came to get me July 2003. It didn't matter what color I was the devil had gotten my "stupid" butt again. I'm divorce, unemployed, back on drugs, homeless, car re-poed, house foreclosed on, being called "bi-polar" while raising my daughter who was seven at the time.

At least "The Prodigal" son was able to remember what he was missing. And came to ...his senses and ...went home...

I had ..."NO SENSE"...left

...to come to or a home to go to...

...no mother or father waiting...

...to greet meet ...

I was now living in the..."Crazy Life"...

Yes I said it!...in the ..."CRAZY HOUSE"...

with more of His "special" sons and daughters.

...Finding "Peace" For Your Journey

He's Adding **"Peace"** To Your Journey
"Today" With

His Mighty Acts of ..."Compassion"...
...for Others...
...He Did It For Them!...
Fed The ...Five Thousand...
*

(Luke 9:10-17)

Upon their return, the apostles reported to Jesus all that they had done. And He took them (along with Him) and withdrew into privacy near a town called Bethsaida. But when the crowds learned of it, (they) followed Him; and He welcomed them and talked to them about the kingdom of God, and healed those who needed restoration to health.

Now the day began to decline, and the Twelve came and said to Him, Dismiss the crowds and send them away, so that they may go to the neighboring hamlets and villages and the surrounding country and find lodging and get a supply of provisions, for we are here in an uninhabited (barren, solitary) place.

But He said to them, You (yourselves) give them (food) to eat. They said, We have no more than five loaves and two fish unless we are to go and buy

food for all this crowd, For there were about 5,000 men. And (Jesus) said to His disciples, Have them (sit down) reclining in table groups (companies) of about fifty each. And they did so, and made them all recline. And taking the five loaves and the two fish,

He looked up to heaven and (praising God) gave thanks and asked Him to bless them (to their use). The He broke them and gave to the disciples to place before the multitude.

And all the people ate and were satisfied. And they gathered up what remained over twelve (small hand) baskets of broken pieces.

*

Thank God ... He Added "Peace" ...To His Journey...

...Finding "Peace" For Your Journey

Day 28

He's Adding **"Peace"** To Your Journey "Today" With

His Mighty Acts of ..."Righteous & Peaceful"... Living
*
(1 Peter 3:8-18)

Finally, be ye all of one mind, having compassion one of another, love as brethren, be pitiful, be courteous: Not rendering evil for evil, or railing for railing: but contrariwise blessing; knowing that ye are thereunto called, that ye should inherit a blessing.

For he that will love life, and see good days, let him refrain his tongue from evil, and his lips that they speak no guile:

Let him eschew evil, and do good; let him

seek peace,

and ensue it. For the eyes of the Lord are over the righteous, and his ears are opened unto their prayers: but the face of the Lord is against them that do evil. And who is he that will harm you, if ye be followers of that which is good?

But and if ye **...suffer...** **for righteousness' sakes** happy are ye: and be not afraid of their terror, neither be troubled. But sanctify the Llord God in your hearts: and be ready always to give an answer to ever man that asketh you, as of evildoers, they may be ashamed that falsely accuse your good conversation in Christ.

For it is better, if the will of God be so, that ye suffer for **well doing,** than for evil doing...

On Your "Faith" Journey
...For Christ also hath once suffered for sins, the just for the unjust, that he might bring us to God, being put to death in the flesh, but quickened by the Spirit...

*

Thank God ... He Added "Peace" ...To His Journey...

...Finding "Peace" For Your Journey

I Encourage You To Go Find A

✱

..."New Quiet Place"...

Like Jesus Did In The

"Garden of Gethsemane"

✱

...And "Ask God" To Help You...

Pray For "PEACE"

...For Yourself ... And Others Today...

...Write Down Three of Your Favorite...

...New... **"Peace"** Scriptures From His Word

✱

..."Great Peace"...
have they which love thy law; and nothing shall offend them

(Psalm 119: 165)

...Finding "Peace" For Your Journey

*This Morning_____

_____
_____
_____
_____
_____

*This Afternoon_____

_____
_____
_____
_____
_____

*This Evening_____

_____
_____
_____
_____
_____

I Believe… I Receive… By Faith…

My God DID_____

"Fifth" Set of Questions...
Are To Help You ..."See"...

"Why"
They Did Not ...Quit!...

What Truly Gave Them ..."PEACE"...

To Keep Them "Moving" In Spite of Their

..."Bitterness & Anger"...
On Their "Faith" Journey?...

I Believe Whatever It Was... God Will Give You What You Need To Keep You Moving If "Bitterness & Anger"

Comes Alone To Make You Quit...

May This Very ..."Powerful Answer"...

Found In The ...Word Of God...

..."Add Peace"...
To Your "Faith" Journey For Life

...Finding "Peace" For Your Journey

They Had What It Took To
..."Please God"...

And He ..."Added"... To Their "Faith"
...What They Needed Daily...

...To Fight The Good Fight Of Faith...
And Finish Their "_____" Journey

When You "See" <u>"Underlined"</u> Words
..."Write Them"...
Down And ..."Meditate On" ...Them For Peace

*(Hebrews 11:6)

_____

_____

_____

But without <u>faith</u> it is <u>impossible</u> to please him: for he that cometh to God must <u>believe</u> that <u>he is</u>, and that he is a <u>rewarder</u> of them that <u>diligently seek him.</u>

*(2 Peter 1:3-8)

_____
_____
_____
_____

According as his <u>divine power</u> hath given unto us all things that pertain unto life and godliness, through the <u>knowledge</u> of him that hath called us to glory in virtue:

Whereby are given unto us <u>exceeding</u> great and precious <u>promises</u>; that by these ye might be partakers of the divine nature, having escaped the corruption that is in the world through lust.

And beside this giving all diligence; add to your "faith" <u>virtue</u>; and to virtue <u>knowledge</u>;

And to knowledge <u>temperance</u>; and to temperance <u>patience</u>; and to patience <u>godliness</u>; And to godliness <u>brotherly kindness</u>; and to brotherly kindness <u>charity</u>.

For if these things be in you; and abound, they make you that ye shall neither be barren nor unfruitful in the knowledge of our Lord Jesus Christ.

...Finding "Peace" For Your Journey

*(Hebrews 10:35-39) amplified

_____
_____
_____
_____

Do not, therefore, fling away your <u>fearless confidence</u>, for it carries a <u>great</u> and <u>glorious</u> compensation of <u>reward.</u>

For you have need of <u>steadfast patience</u> and <u>endurance,</u> so that you may <u>perform</u> and fully <u>accomplish</u> the <u>will of God</u>, and thus <u>receive</u> and carry away (and enjoy to the full) what is promised.

For still a little while (a very little while), and the coming one will come and He will come and

He will not delay.

But the just shall <u>live</u> by <u>faith</u> (My righteous servant shall live by his <u>conviction</u> respecting man's <u>relationship</u> to God and <u>divine</u> things, and holy fervor <u>born</u> of faith and <u>conjoined</u> with it); and if he <u>draws back</u> and shrinks in <u>fear,</u> My soul has no <u>delight</u> of <u>pleasure</u> in him. But our way is not that of those who draw back to eternal misery (perdition) and are utterly <u>destroyed,</u> but we are of those who <u>believe</u> (who cleave to and <u>trust</u> in and <u>rely</u> on <u>God through Jesus Christ,</u> the Messiah) and by faith preserve our soul.

*(2Timothy 4:6-8) amplified

For I am already about to be sacrificed (<u>my life</u> is about to be <u>poured out</u> as a drink offering); the time of my (spirit's) release (from the body) is at hand and I will soon go <u>free.</u>

_____
_____
_____

I have <u>fought</u> the good, (worthy, honorable, and noble) <u>fight,</u> I have <u>finished</u> the race, I have <u>kept</u> (firmly held) the <u>faith</u>....

_____
_____
_____

Henceforth there is <u>laid up</u> for me <u>a crown</u> of <u>righteousness,</u> which the Lord, the righteous <u>judge,</u> shall <u>give me</u> at that day: and not to me only, but unto <u>all them</u> also that <u>love his appearing.</u>

_____
_____
_____

...Finding "Peace" For Your Journey

He's Adding **"Peace"** To My Journey

"Today" By **"Showing Me"**

Why **"Jesus"** Didn't Quit...

He Cared More About ..."Pleasing His Father" ...
Who Desired To "Save of Us All" Through The Birth,
Burial & Resurrection of His Son ...Jesus Christ...

(Philippians 2:1-11) amplified

SO BY whatever (appeal to you there is in our mutual dwelling in Christ, by whatever) strengthening and consoling and encouraging (our relationship) in Him (affords), by whatever persuasive incentive there is in love, by whatever participation in the (Holy) Spirit (we share), and by whatever depth of affection and compassionate sympathy,

Fill up and complete my joy by living in harmony and being of the same mind and one in purpose. having the same love, being in full accord and of one harmonious mind and intention.

Do nothing from factional motives

(through contentiousness, strife, selfishness, or for unworthy ends) or prompted by conceit and empty arrogance, Instead,

in the true spirit of humility

(lowliness of mind)

let each regard the others

as better than and superior to himself

(thinking more highly of one another than

you do of yourselves).

Let each of you esteem and look upon and be concerned for not (merely) his own interests, but also each for the interests of others.

Let this same attitude and purpose and (humble) mind be in you which was in Christ Jesus:

Let Him be your example in (humility;)

Who, although being essentially one with God and in

the form of God (possessing the fullness of the attributes which make God), did not think this equality with God was a thing to be eagerly grasped or retained.

But stripped Himself

(of all privileges and rightful dignity), so as to assume the guise of a servant (slave), in that He became like men and was born a human being.

And after He had appeared in human form, He abased and humbled Himself (still further) and carried

*

His obedience to the extreme of death,

even the death of the cross!

Therefore (because He stooped so low)

God has highly exalted Him and has freely bestowed on Him the name that is above every name.

That in (at) the name of Jesus every knee should (must) bow, in heaven and on earth under the earth,

And every tongue (frankly and openly) confess and acknowledge that Jesus Christ is Lord,

to the glory of God the Father.

Therefore, my dear ones, as you have always obeyed (my suggestions), so now, not only (with the enthusiasm you would show) in my presence but much more because I am absent, work out (cultivate, carry out to the goal, and fully complete)

...your own salvation...

with reverence and awe trembling (self-distrust with serious caution, tenderness of conscience, watchfulness against temptation, timidly shrinking from whatever might offend God and discredit the name of Christ).

(Not in your own strength) for it is God Who is all the while effectually at work in you (energizing and creating in you the power and desire), both to will and to work for His good pleasure and satisfaction and delight.

Do all things without grumbling and faulting and complaining (against God) and question and doubting (among yourselves).

That you may show yourselves to be **...blameless...** and guileless innocent and uncontaminated; children of God without blemish (faultless, unrebukable) in the midst of a crooked and wicked generation (spiritually perverted and perverse), among whom you are seen as bright lights, (stars or beacons shining out clearly) in the **...(dark) world...** Holding out (to it) and offering (to all men) the Word of Life, so that in the day of Christ I may have something of which exultantly, to rejoice and glory in that I did not run my race in vain of spend my labor to **...no purpose...**

...Finding "Peace" For Your Journey

<u>There Is So Much "PEACE" To Be Found In Reading That "Powerful Scripture"</u>

Can You "See" Why It Was So Important For "Jesus"

...To Finish His "Faith" Journey?...

And Walk In "Humility & Righteousness"

_____
_____
_____
_____
_____

Why Is It Important That You To Do The Same?

..."Finish" Your "Faith" Journey...With God

_____
_____
_____
_____

I Believe... I Receive... By Faith...

My God CAN_____

...Finding "Peace" For Your Journey

Why "Abraham" Didn't Quit...

He Cared More About "Pleasing His Father" ...
Who Had "Promised Him" Great Things, Before
He Died ... Including A Son

(Genesis 12:1-11) amplified
Now (in Haran) the Lord said to Abram, Go for
yourself (for your own advantage) away from your
country, from your relatives and your father's house, to
the land that I will show you.

And I will make you a great nation, and I will bless
you (with abundant increase of favors) and make your
name famous and distinguished, and you will be a
blessing (dispensing good to others).

And I will bless those who bless you (who confer
prosperity or happiness upon you) and curse him who
curses of uses insolent language toward you; in you
will all the families and kindred of the earth be blessed
(and by you the will bless themselves)

...Finding "Peace" For Your Journey

So **Abram** departed,... as the Lord had **directed him;** and Lot (his nephew) went with, Abram was seventy five years old when he left Haran...

To "Finish" Not Start...His "Faith" Journey
...With God...

...On A "Promise"...
He Had From The Lord...

- Read Genesis Chapter 18:1-15 ...
To See What God "Promised" Him

- Read Genesis Chapter 21:1-7 ...
To See The "Promised Child" Came At Age 100

...Finding "Peace" For Your Journey

He's Adding **"Peace"** To My Journey

"Today" By **"Showing Me"**

Why **"Jacob"** Didn't Quit...

He Cared More About Pleasing "Himself"
...Instead of His Father...
God Used His...Good...Bad... & His Ugly...
To Please "Himself" & "Bless" Us All

(Genesis 28:10- 14)

And Jacob went out from Beer-sheba, and went toward Haran. And he lighted upon a certain place, and tarried there all night, because the sun was set; and he took of the stones of that place, and put them for his pillows, and lay down in that place to sleep.

And he dreamed, and behold a ladder set up on the earth, and the top of it reached to heaven: and behold the angles of God ascending and descending on it.

And, behold, the Lord stood above it, and said,
I am the LORD God of Abram thy father, and the God
of Isaac: the land whereon thou liest, to thee will I give
it, and to thy seed;

And thy seed shall be as the dust of the earth, and
thou shalt spread abroad to the west, and to the east,
and to the north, and to the south: and in thee and in
thy seed shall all the families
of the earth be blessed.

And, behold, I am with thee, and will keep thee in all
places whither thou goest, and will bring thee again
into this land; for I will not leave thee, until I have
done that which I have spoken to thee of.

And Jacob rose up early in the morning, and took the
stone that he had put for his pillows, and set it up for
a pillar, and poured oil upon the top of it.

And he called the name of that place Beth-el: but the
name of the city was called Luz at the first.

And Jacob vowed a vow, saying, If God will be with
me, and will keep me in this way that I go and will
give me bread to eat, and raiment to put on. So that I
come again to my father's house in PEACE; then shall

the LORD be my God:

And this stone, which I have set for a pillar, shall be

God's house: and of all that thou shalt give me I will

...surely give the tenth unto thee...

As He "Presses On" To...**"Finish"**...
...Not Quit or Start Over...
On His ..."Now Faith"... Journey With God

...On A "Vow"...
He Made Unto The Lord

*

It's Easy To "See" Why He's

Well Known To Many As

...The Bad Boy...Trickster...Swindler

...Finding "Peace" For Your Journey

But, "Called & Used" By God...

He Got "Played" By His Uncle (Laban)

- Read Genesis "Chapter 27" ...To see Jacob's Tricks, Steals Him A Blessing

- Read Genesis "Chapter 28" ...To see Jacob's Dream Gets Him Before "His God

- Read Genesis "Chapter 29" ...To see Jacob's Heart's Desire His "Pretty" Wife Read Genesis "Chapter 31"... To see Jacob's Payback... From Labon And God...

- Read Genesis "Chapter 32" ...To see Jacob's Wrestling For A Greater Blessing

...When You Read His Story... You Will Soon "See" ...How "God's Word"...

Can "Change" Your Life...Your Name...
And "Use" Your "Faith" Journey To
...Please HIM...

...Finding "Peace" For Your Journey

Why "Joseph" Didn't Quit...

He Cared More About Pleasing The Giver of
"His Dream" ...The Father...
And His Brothers Cared More About "Killing"
...The Dreamer of The Dream...

(Genesis 37:3-8)

Now Israel loved Joseph more than all his children, because he was the son of his old age: and he made him a coat of many colors.

And when his brethren saw that their father loved him more that all his brethren, the hated him, and could **not speak peaceable**... unto him.

And Joseph dreamed a dream, and he told his brethren: and they hated him yet the more.

And he said unto them, hear, I pray you, this dream which I have dreamed:

For, behold, we were binding sheaves in the field, and lo, my sheaf arose, and also stood upright; and, behold, your sheaves stood round about, and made obeisance

to my sheaf.
And his brenthren said to him, Shalt thou indeed reign over us? or shalt thou indeed have dominion over us? And they hated him yet the more for his dreams, and for his words.

His Brothers ...Envied Him ... But, His God ...Favored Him...
As They "Watched" Him ...Go From The - Pit To The - Palace....
"Finish"
...His "Faith" Journey...Bring Glory To God...

Fulfilling ..."His Dream"... From ...The Lord...

- Read Genesis "Chapter 41"...To See The Dreamer Moves ...From The Pit To The Place

- Read Genesis "Chapter 44"...To See The Dreamer Makes A "Forgiveness" Cup

- Read Genesis "Chapter 45"...To See The Dreamer Reveal His Identity & Power

- Read Genesis "Chapter 47"...To See The Dreamer Care For His Haters...

...Finding "Peace" For Your Journey

Day 31

He's Adding **"Peace"** To My Journey "Today" By **"Showing Me"**

Why **"Ruth"** Didn't Quit...

She Cared More About Staying With The Woman
...Who Was "Trusting God"...
To Care For Her "Every" Need... And They Received
"Favor & Blessings" ... From God

(Read The Book of Ruth)

...only 5 short chapters...

This story is known as a beautiful "Love Story" between the Handsome, Wealthy Boaz and the Beautiful Broke young woman Ruth that found "Favor" in his sight. Her mother –n law Naomi had lost both her husband and her two sons, one was married to Ruth.

She now has to trust God even more to add peace to her "Faith" Journey daily to keep her moving in spite of her bitterness and anger about the lost of the men that once provided for them all. She tried to encourage Ruth to go back to her family to get her needs met, so Ruth would not have to "Trust God" with her. . But, instead look at what Ruth said: in ....(1:16-17)

And Ruth said, Urge me not to leave you or to turn back from following you; for where you go I will go, and where you lodge I will lodge. Your people shall be my people and your God my God. Where you die I will die, and there will I be buried. The Lord do so to me, and more also, if anything but death parts me from you.
So Boaz took Ruth, and she was his wife; and when he went in unto her, the Lord gave her conception, and she bare a son.
And the women said unto Naomi, Blessed be the LORD, which hath not left thee this day without a kinsman, that his name may be unto thee a restorer of thy life, and a nourisher of thine old age: for thy daughter-in-law, which loveth thee, which is better to thee than seven, hath borne him............(4:13-15)
"Agape Love"... Help Them "Finish & Start" Their "Faith" Journey With God...And Provided Wealth And More Love For Their Future...

...Finding "Peace" For Your Journey

Why "Ester" Didn't Quit...

(Read The Book of Ester)

...only 9 short chapters...

She Cared More About Helping Her God "Save" Her People...Than Helping Her Husband Be "Happy" And Her God Be Sad He Even Chose Her...

*

Well like Ruth, Ester was fair and beautiful. A real "nobody predestined for greatness." Raised by her uncle Mordecai. The heart of the story is the King desired a new "submissive" wife and Ester was chosen to replace the old disobedient Queen. When Ester obeyed "God's Assignment" to marry, she didn't know it included risking her life to save God's Chosen people (The Jews.)   (chapter 2:15, 17)

And Ester obtained favour in the sight of all them that looked upon her. The King loved Ester above all the women, and she obtained grace and favour in his sight more than all the virgins; so that he set the royal crown upon her head, and made her queen instead of Vashti.

Just like the enemy to come and try to mess up her good "God Thing".

(chapter 3:13)

And letters were sent by posts into all the king's provinces, to destroy, to kill and to cause to perish, all Jews, both young and old, little children and women

(chapter 7:3)

Then Ester the queen answered and said, If I have found favour in thy sight, O king, and if it please the king, let my life be given me at my petition, and my people at my request...

Let Us "Finish"
Our ..."Faith"... Journey With God
On A ..."Saving Word"...
...From Our King ...

...Finding "Peace" For Your Journey

He's Adding **"Peace"** To My Journey "Today" By **"Showing Me"**

Why **"Mary"** Didn't Quit...

She Cared More About "Believing" In The "Living Word" She Carried For Nine Months...Than "Crying" Over The Son Who Had To Die For Others To Live...

(Luke 1:26-35)

And in the sixth month the angel Gabriel was sent from God unto a city of Galilee, named Nazareth. To a virgin espoused to a man whose name was Joseph, of the house of David; and the virgin's name was Mary.

And the angel came in unto her, and said, Hail, thou that art highly favoured, the Lord is with thee, blessed art thou among women. And when she saw him, she was troubled at his saying, and cast in her mind what manner of salutation this should be. And the angel said unto her Fear not, Mary: for thou hast found favour with God.

And, behold, thou shalt conceive in thy womb, and bring forth a son, and shalt call his name JESUS. He shall be great, and shall be called the Son of the Highest: and the And Lord God shall give unto him the throne of his father David. And he shall reign over the house of Jacob for ever; and of his kingdom there shall be no end.

Then said Mary unto the angel, How shall this be, seeing I know not a man. And the angel answered and said unto her, The Holy Ghost shall come upon thee, and the power of the Highest shall overshadow thee: therefore also that holy thing which shall be born of thee shall be called the Son of God.

For with God nothing shall be impossible. And Mary said, Behold the handmaid of the Lord; be it unto me according to thy word, the angel departed from her.

*

So she …"Finished"…Her "Faith" Journey With God Carrying The "Word of God" In Her "Chosen Body" …She Was A Gift of "Healing" From God…

...Finding "Peace" For Your Journey

"Sixth" Set of Questions...

Are To Help You See "How"...

"Easy"

...It Is To Become...

A "Christian"...

A "Follower"...

of Christ

...On Your "Faith" Journey...

...Finding "Peace" For Your Journey

Is This The ..."Beginning"... or The "End" of Your "Faith Walk"

...With The LORD?...

This
...Is...
The
Beginning

...Finding "Peace" For Your Journey

or Could This Be The …"End?"…

Your Last "Chance" To Commit Today…

To Walking Out "Your Last"… Days With

Jesus Christ As Your Savoir…

…And…

This

Could Be

...Finding "Peace" For Your Journey

In This Moment Do You Feel The "Power of God" Right Now? No Matter …Where You Are?

---

*

In "His Presence" is Fullness of Joy

The End

of

This

Powerful

...Finding "Peace" For Your Journey

Can You See Yourself "Writing" A Powerful
...Little Book?...

---

or Telling Others...About How God "Saved"
You... From A Life of Sin...

Beautiful

Little

...Book...

of

"Words"

...Finding "Peace" For Your Journey

Do You Believe That "Words" Are Powerful?...

Are Any of These "Words" Encouraging You

To Call ...Upon The Lord...

Just To Tell Him "Thank You"... For All His Done
...For You So Far?...

...Scriptures ...

To

"HelpU"

...Finding "Peace" For Your Journey

Do You Believe That This "Little Book" Is In Your ...Hands By Accident?...

Or Was It "Predestined" To Arrive To You

On This Very Special Day _____

...To...

Lead You

To

...Christ...

So That

Who Do You Think Sent It To You... For Real?

...Finding "Peace" For Your Journey

Who Do You Know…That Cares This Much

…For You…

Has Anyone "Died" For You Lately? So…

You

Can Be

…Saved…

By

"His Grace"

Would You Like To Know Why The "Word of God"…

...Finding "Peace" For Your Journey

Is Coming To "Give You" The … "Answers"…
To These Few …"Simple" But, …

Powerful "Questions" In This Little Book… That Is Showing Up On "Your Journey" At This "Appointed" Time …In Your Life…

This Is "How"

The

…WORD…

Became

"Flesh"

According To The Gospel Of St. John (1:1-18)

IN THE beginning

was the Word, and the Word was with God

and the Word was God.

The same was in the beginning with God.

All things were made by him; and without him was not anything made that was made.

In him was life; and the life was the light of men.

And the light shineth in darkness; and the darkness comprehended it not.

There was a man sent from God, whose name was John.

The same came for a witness, to bear witness of that Light, that all men through him might believe.

He was not that Light, but was sent to bear witness of that Light.

That was the true Light, which lighteth every man that cometh in the world.

He was in the world, and the world was made by him, and the world knew him not;

He came unto his own, and his own received him not,.

But as many as received him, to them gave he power to become the sons of God, even to them that believe on his name.

...Finding "Peace" For Your Journey

Which were born, not of blood, nor of the will of the flesh, nor of the will of man, but of God.

And the Word was made flesh, and dwelt among us, (and we beheld his glory, the glory as of the only begotten of the Father,) full of grace and truth.

John bare witness of him, and cried, saying, This was he of whom I spake, He that cometh after me is preferred before me: for he was before me.

And of his **fullness** have all we received, and grace for grace.
For the law was given by Moses, but grace and truth came by

...Jesus Christ...

...Finding "Peace" For Your Journey

No man hath seen God at any time; the only begotten Son, Which is in the bosom of the Father, he hath declared him.

---

ow...Do You See Why It's So
"Important"

That You "Invite"

...Jesus...

...The "Living Word" of God...

To "Travel" With You Right Now?

To "Add" A Little "PEACE"

To Your ..."Faith" Journey... "Daily?"

...In Your "Time" of Need...

May You "Always" Look To

...Father God...

To "Give" You

- ➢ Strength ...For Your Journey
- ➢ Peace ...For Your Journey
- ➢ Hope ...For Your Journey
- ➢ Courage ...For Your Journey
- ➢ Joy ...For Your Journey

As You "Read" One of These Powerful Little "Imperfect" Books ... About Our

..."Perfect" Savior...

His ..."Word Will Perfect"... You Daily!

...Finding "Peace" For Your Journey

To
...God...
Be
...The...
"Glory"

...For Inspiring Me To...
Write About
...His Story & My Story!...
...I Pray By Now ...

...Finding "Peace" For Your Journey

...You...
Are
"Ready"
To Be # "Born"
...Again...
If You Are Not Already

✶

A "Born Again" Christian

...Finding "Peace" For Your Journey

...That at the "name" of... "Jesus" every knee should bow, of things in heaven, and things in earth, and things under the earth;

and that every tongue should confess that "Jesus" ...Christ... is Lord, to the glory of God ...the Father...
(Philippians 2:10-11)

According To Your "Word"

(Revelation 3:20)

Behold, I stand at the door, and "knock" if any man hear my voice and "open" the door, I will "come in" to him, and will "sup with him, and he with me."

LORD, I "Invite"
..."Jesus Christ"...
Into My Life
On This Very ..."Special Day"...

Thank You Father God ... For "Adding" A Little

"Peace"

To My "Faith" Journey

...Finding "Peace" For Your Journey

"Father God"
May You Always "Add" A Little
..."PEACE"...
To My "Faith" Journey
Every Time I "Confess"..."Your Word"... To You!

_____
_____
_____
_____
_____
_____
_____
_____
_____
_____
_____
_____
_____
_____
_____
_____
_____

Write A Few "Favorite Scriptures"...To Confess In Prayer!

"Father God"
May I Always ..."Show You"... How Much
...I "Love" You...
And How "Thankful" I Am That You "Sent" Your Son
..."Jesus"... To Die For Me And My Sins

_____
_____
_____
_____
_____
_____
_____
_____
_____
_____
_____
_____
_____
_____
_____
_____
_____
_____
_____
_____
_____
_____

Write A Special ..."Love"... Letter To "Your" Father

...Finding "Peace" For Your Journey

"Father God"
May You Always "Add" A Little
..."PEACE"...To My Heart To "Remove"
**All "Bitterness & Anger"
That I May Have ..."Hidden Deep"... Inside
Towards These People ... I Feel Have ..."Hurt Me"
While Traveling ... On My "Faith" Journey**

_____
_____
_____
_____
_____
_____
_____
_____
_____
_____
_____
_____
_____
_____
_____
_____

Help Me To Always Walk In ..."Love & Forgiveness"...

...Finding "Peace" For Your Journey

"Father God"
Here's How ... I Know ... That I Know...
I Have Your "Peace" Today!

_____
_____
_____
_____
_____
_____
_____
_____
_____
_____
_____
_____
_____
_____
_____
_____
_____

_ Help Me To Always Walk In ..."Love & Forgiveness"...

...Finding "Peace" For Your Journey

...Finding "Peace" For Your Journey

...Finding "Peace" For Your Journey

"Spiritual" Things I Want To
..."Meditate On"...
..."Power2Press"... Notes For Me To
"Remember"... About My "Faith" Journey...

_____
_____
_____
_____
_____
_____
_____
_____
_____
_____
_____
_____
_____
_____
_____
_____
_____
_____
_____
_____
_____
_____

LORD... Order My "Steps" In Your ..."Word"...

...Finding "Peace" For Your Journey

*Holy Spirit ... "Help Me" ..."Meditate On"...

...Finding "Peace" For Your Journey

*Holy Spirit ... "Help Me" ..."Meditate On"...

...Finding "Peace" For Your Journey

*Holy Spirit ... "Help Me" ..."Meditate On"...

*My "Instructions & Visions"... From The LORD!

*My "Instructions & Visions"… From The LORD!

...Finding "Peace" For Your Journey

"Power2Press"... Notes For Me To ..."Remember"...

"Power2Press"... Notes For Me To ..."Remember"...

...Finding "Peace" For Your Journey

How Did This Little ..."Imperfect"...
"Book"
...Help You Find...
"Peace" For Your Journey?

_____
_____
_____
_____
_____
_____
_____
_____
_____
_____
_____
_____
_____
_____
_____
_____
_____
_____

Please ..."Let Us Know" ...
E-mail ... Power2Press@yahoo.com

...Finding "Peace" For Your Journey